Ace the CLEP College Algebra in 30 Days

www.EffortlessMath.com

... So Much More Online!

✓ FREE Math lessons

✓ More Math learning books!

✓ Mathematics Worksheets

✓ Online Math Tutors

Need a PDF version of this book?

Please visit www.EffortlessMath.com

Ace the CLEP College Algebra in 30 Days

The Ultimate Crash Course to Beat the CLEP College Algebra Test

By

Reza Nazari

& Ava Ross

Copyright © 2019

Reza Nazari & Ava Ross

All rights reserved. No part of this publication may be reproduced, stored in a retrieval system, or transmitted in any form or by any means, electronic, mechanical, photocopying, recording, scanning, or otherwise, except as permitted under Section 107 or 108 of the 1976 United States Copyright Act, without permission of the author.

All inquiries should be addressed to:

info@effortlessMath.com

www.EffortlessMath.com

ISBN−13: 978-1-64612-156-4

ISBN−10: 1-64612-156-2

Published by: Effortless Math Education

www.EffortlessMath.com

Description

The goal of this book is simple. It will help you incorporate the most effective method and the right strategies to prepare for the CLEP College Algebra test quickly and effectively.

Ace the CLEP College Algebra in 30 Days, which reflects the 2019 test guidelines and topics, is designed to help you hone your math skills, overcome your exam anxiety, and boost your confidence - and do your best to defeat CLEP College Algebra Test. This CLEP College Algebra new edition has been updated to replicate questions appearing on the most recent CLEP College Algebra tests. This is a precious learning tool for CLEP College Algebra test takers who need extra practice in math to improve their CLEP College Algebra score. After reviewing this book, you will have solid foundation and adequate practice that is necessary to ace the CLEP College Algebra test. **This book is your ticket to ace the CLEP College Algebra!**

Ace the CLEP College Algebra in 30 Days provides students with the confidence and math skills they need to succeed on the CLEP College Algebra, providing a solid foundation of basic Math topics with abundant exercises for each topic. It is designed to address the needs of CLEP College Algebra test takers who must have a working knowledge of basic Math.

Inside the pages of this comprehensive book, students can learn math topics in a structured manner with a complete study program to help them understand essential math skills. It also has many exciting features, including:

- Content 100% aligned with the 2019 CLEP College Algebra test
- Written by CLEP College Algebra tutors and test experts
- Complete coverage of all CLEP College Algebra concepts and topics which you will be tested
- Step-by-step guide for all CLEP College Algebra topics
- Dynamic design and easy-to-follow activities
- Over 2,500 additional CLEP College Algebra practice questions in both multiple-choice and grid-in formats with answers grouped by topic, so you can focus on your weak areas
- Abundant Math skill building exercises to help test-takers approach different question types that might be unfamiliar to them
- Exercises on different CLEP College Algebra topics such as integers, percent, equations, polynomials, exponents and radicals
- 2 full-length practice tests (featuring new question types) with detailed answers
- Effortlessly and confidently follow the step-by-step instructions in this book to ace the College Math Placement in a short period of time.

***CLEP College Algebra in 30 Days* is the only book you'll ever need to master Basic Math topics!** It can be used as a self-study course - you do not need to work with a Math tutor. (It can also be used with a Math tutor).

You'll be surprised how fast you master the Math topics covering on CLEP College Algebra Test. **Ideal for self-study as well as for classroom usage.**

About the Author

Reza Nazari is the author of more than 100 Math learning books including:
– **Math and Critical Thinking Challenges:** For the Middle and High School Student
– **GRE Math in 30 Days**
– **ASVAB Math Workbook 2018 - 2019**
– **Effortless Math Education Workbooks**
– and many more Mathematics books …

Reza is also an experienced Math instructor and a test–prep expert who has been tutoring students since 2008. Reza is the founder of Effortless Math Education, a tutoring company that has helped many students raise their standardized test scores—and attend the colleges of their dreams. Reza provides an individualized custom learning plan and the personalized attention that makes a difference in how students view math.

You can contact Reza via email at:
reza@EffortlessMath.com

Find Reza's professional profile at:
goo.gl/zoC9rJ

Contents

Day 1: Order of Operations and Scientific Notation 10
    Order of Operations 11
    Scientific Notation 12
    Answers – Day 1 13

Day 2: Exponents Operations and Sets 14
    Exponents Operations 15
    Sets 16
    Answers – Day 2 17

Day 3: Algebraic Expressions 18
    Evaluating Expressions 19
    Simplifying Algebraic Expressions 20
    Answers – Day 3 21

Day 4: Equations 22
    One–Step Equations 23
    Multi–Step Equations 24
    Answers – Day 4 25

Day 5: Inequalities 26
    Graphing Single–Variable Inequalities 27
    One–Step Inequalities 28
    Answers – Day 5 29

Day 6: Multi–Step Inequalities 30
    Multi–Step Inequalities 31
    Answers – Day 6 32

Day 7: System of Equations 33
    Systems of Equations 34
    Systems of Equations Word Problems 35
    Answers – Day 7 36

Day 8: Quadratic 37
    Solving a Quadratic Equation 38

    Graphing Quadratic Functions 39

    Answers – Day 8 40

Day 9: Quadratic Inequalities 41

    Solving Quadratic Inequalities 42

    Graphing Quadratic inequalities 43

    Answers – Day 9 44

Day 10: Complex Numbers 45

    Adding and Subtracting Complex Numbers 46

    Multiplying and Dividing Complex Numbers 47

    Answers – Day 10 48

Day 11: Imaginary Numbers and Polynomials 49

    Rationalizing Imaginary Denominators 50

    Writing Polynomials in Standard Form 51

    Answers – Day 11 52

Day 12: Adding and Subtracting Polynomials 53

    Simplifying Polynomials 54

    Adding and Subtracting Polynomials 55

    Answers – Day 12 56

Day 13: Multiplying and Dividing Monomials 57

    Multiplying Monomials 58

    Multiplying and Dividing Monomials 59

    Answers – Day 13 60

Day 14: Monomials and Binomials 61

    Multiplying a Polynomial and a Monomial 62

    Multiplying Binomials 63

    Answers – Day 14 64

Day 15: Operations with Polynomials 65

    Factoring Trinomials 66

    Operations with Polynomials 67

    Answers – Day 15 68

Day 16: Functions 69

    Function Notation 70

Adding and Subtracting Functions 71

Answers – Day 16 72

Day 17: Multiplying and Dividing Functions 73

Multiplying and Dividing Functions 74

Composition of Functions 75

Answers – Day 17 76

Day 18: Logarithms 77

Evaluating Logarithms 78

Properties of Logarithms 79

Answers – Day 18 80

Day 19: Natural Logarithms 81

Natural Logarithms 82

Solving Logarithmic Equations 83

Answers – Day 19 84

Day 20: Radical Expressions 85

Simplifying Radical Expressions 86

Simplifying Radical Expressions Involving Fractions 87

Answers – Day 20 88

Day 21: Radical Expressions Operations 89

Multiplying Radical Expressions 90

Adding and Subtracting Radical Expressions 91

Answers – Day 21 92

Day 22: Radical Functions 93

Domain and Range of Radical Functions 94

Radical Equations 95

Answers – Day 22 96

Day 23: Rational Expressions 97

Simplifying Rational Expressions 98

Graphing Rational Expressions 99

Answers – Day 23 100

Day 24: Multiplying and Dividing Rational Expressions 101

Multiplying Rational Expressions 102

Dividing Rational Expressions 103

Answers – Day 24 104

Day 25: Adding and Subtracting Rational Expressions 105

Adding and Subtracting Rational Expressions 106

Rational Equations 107

Answers – Day 25 108

Day 26: Complex Fractions 109

Simplify Complex Fractions 110

Answers – Day 26 111

Day 27: Arithmetic and Geometric Sequences 112

Arithmetic Sequences 113

Geometric Sequences 114

Answers – Day 27 115

Day 28: Finite and Infinite Geometric Series 116

Finite Geometric Series 117

Infinite Geometric Series 118

Answers – Day 28 119

Day 29: Time to Test 120

Day 30: A Realistic CLEP College Algebra Test 148

Day 1: Order of Operations and Scientific Notation

Topics that you'll learn today:

- ✓ The Order of Operations
- ✓ Scientific Notation

"A Man is like a fraction whose numerator is what he is and whose denominator is what he thinks of himself. The larger the denominator, the smaller the fraction." –Tolstoy

Order of Operations

Step-by-step guide:

When there is more than one math operation, use PEMDAS:

- ✓ Parentheses
- ✓ Exponents
- ✓ Multiplication and Division (from left to right)
- ✓ Addition and Subtraction (from left to right)

Examples:

1) Solve. $(2 + 4) \div (2^2 \div 4) =$

   First simplify inside parentheses: $(6) \div (4 \div 4) = (6) \div (1) =$
   Then: $(6) \div (1) = 6$

2) Solve. $(9 \times 6) - (10 - 6) =$

   First simplify inside parentheses: $(9 \times 6) - (10 - 6) = (54) - (4) =$

   Then: $(54) - (4) = 50$

✎ *Evaluate each expression.*

1) $12 + (3 \times 2) =$

2) $8 - (4 \times 5) =$

3) $(8 \times 2) + 14 =$

4) $(10 - 6) - (4 \times 3) =$

5) $15 + (12 \div 2) =$

6) $(24 \times 3) \div 4 =$

7) $(28 \div 2) \times (-4) =$

8) $(2 \times 6) + (14 - 8) =$

9) $45 + (4 \times 2) + 12 =$

10) $(10 \times 5) \div (4 + 1) =$

11) $(-6) + (8 \times 6) + 10 =$

12) $(12 \times 4) - (56 \div 4) =$

Scientific Notation

Step-by-step guide:

- ✓ It is used to write very big or very small numbers in decimal form.
- ✓ In scientific notation all numbers are written in the form of:

$$m \times 10^n$$

Decimal notation	Scientific notation
5	5×10^0
$-25,000$	-2.5×10^4
0.5	5×10^{-1}
2,122.456	$2,122456 \times 10^{-3}$

Example:

1) **Write 0.00015 in scientific notation.**

   First, move the decimal point to the right so that you have a number that is between 1 and 10. Then: $N = 1.5$

   Second, determine how many places the decimal moved in step 1 by the power of 10. Then: 10^{-4} → When the decimal moved to the right, the exponent is negative. Then: $0.00015 = 1.5 \times 10^{-4}$

2) **Write 9.5×10^{-5} in standard notation.**

   10^{-5} → When the decimal moved to the right, the exponent is negative.
   Then: $9.5 \times 10^{-5} = 0.000095$

✍ *Write each number in scientific notation.*

1) $15,000,000 =$

2) $67,000 =$

3) $0.000819 =$

4) $0.00092 =$

✍ *Write each number in standard notation.*

5) $4.5 \times 10^3 =$

6) $8 \times 10^{-4} =$

7) $6 \times 10^{-1} =$

8) $9 \times 10^{-2} =$

Answers – Day 1

Order of Operations

1) 18
2) −12
3) 30
4) −8
5) 21
6) 18
7) −56
8) 18
9) 65
10) 10
11) 52
12) 34

Scientific Notation

1) 1.5×10^7
2) 6.7×10^4
3) 8.19×10^{-4}
4) 9.2×10^{-4}
5) 4,500
6) 0.0008
7) 0.6
8) 0.09

Day 2: Exponents Operations and Sets

Topics that you'll learn today:

- ✓ Exponents Operations
- ✓ Sets

Mathematics is an art of human understanding. ~ William Thurston

Exponents Operations

Step-by-step guide:

- ✓ Exponents are shorthand for repeated multiplication of the same number by itself. For example, instead of 2×2, we can write 2^2. For $3 \times 3 \times 3 \times 3$, we can write 3^4
- ✓ In algebra, a variable is a letter used to stand for a number. The most common letters are: $x, y, z, a, b, c, m,$ and n.
- ✓ Exponent's rules: $x^a \times x^b = x^{a+b}$, $\frac{x^a}{x^b} = x^{a-b}$

$$(x^a)^b = x^{a \times b}, \qquad (xy)^a = x^a \times y^a, \left(\frac{a}{b}\right)^c = \frac{a^c}{b^c}$$

Examples:

1) **Multiply.** $4x^3 \times 2x^2 =$

   Use Exponent's rules: $x^a \times x^b = x^{a+b} \rightarrow x^3 \times x^2 = x^{3+2} = x^5$

   Then: $4x^3 \times 2x^2 = 8x^5$

2) **Multiply.** $(x^3 y^5)^2 =$

   Use Exponent's rules: $(x^a)^b = x^{a \times b}$. Then: $(x^3 y^5)^2 = x^{3 \times 2} y^{5 \times 2} = x^6 y^{10}$

✎ *Simplify and write the answer in exponential form.*

1) $2x^2 \times 4x =$

2) $5x^4 \times x^2 =$

3) $8x^4 \times 3x^5 =$

4) $3x^2 \times 6xy =$

5) $2x^5 y \times 4x^2 y^3 =$

6) $9x^2 y^5 \times 5x^2 y^8 =$

7) $5x^2 y \times 5x^2 y^7 =$

8) $7x^6 \times 3x^9 y^4 =$

9) $8x^8 y^5 \times 7x^5 y^3 =$

10) $9x^6 x^2 \times 4xy^5 =$

11) $12xy^7 \times 2x^9 y^8 =$

12) $9x^9 y^{12} \times 9x^{14} y^{11} =$

Sets

Step-by-step guide:

- ✓ A set is a collection of objects and each object is an "element" in the set.
- ✓ Set Notation: A set is denoted by a capital letter, such as A, B, or C etc. The list of a set elements enclosed in braces: {...}
- ✓ Set Operations: The union (with the sing ∪) of two sets is the set of elements that belong to one or both of the two sets. The intersection of two sets (with the sing ∩) is the set of elements that are common to both sets.

Example:

1) If A = {2, 5, 11, 15}, B = {1, 2, 3, 4, 5, 6}, and C = {5, 7, 9, 11, 13}, then which of the following set is (A ∪ B) ∩ C?

   A. {1, 2, 3, 4, 5, 6, 11, 15}
   B. {1, 2, 3, 4, 5, 6, 7, 11, 13, 15}
   C. {5, 11, 13, 15}
   D. {5, 11}

Answer: Choice D is correct. The union of A and B is: A ∪ B = {1, 2, 3, 4, 5, 6, 11, 15}
The intersection of (A ∪ B) and C is: (A ∪ B) ∩ C = {5, 11}, because only 5 and 11 are common to both sets of (A ∪ B) and C.

Given $A = \{1, 2, 3, 8, 12\}$, $B = \{2, 4, 5, 7\}$, and $C = \{5, 7, 9, 11\}$, find:

1) A ∪ B _____

2) A ∪ C _____

3) B ∪ C _____

4) A ∩ B _____

5) A ∩ C _____

6) B ∩ C _____

7) (A ∪ B) ∪ C _____

8) (A ∪ B) ∩ C _____

9) (A ∩ B) ∩ C _____

10) (B ∪ C) ∩ A _____

Answers – Day 2

Exponents Operations

1) $8x^3$
2) $5x^6$
3) $24x^9$
4) $18x^3y$
5) $8x^7y^4$
6) $45x^4y^{13}$
7) $25x^4y^8$
8) $21x^{15}y^4$
9) $56x^{13}y^8$
10) $36x^9y^5$
11) $24x^{10}y^{15}$
12) $81x^{23}y^{23}$

Sets

1) $\{1, 2, 3, 4, 5, 7, 8, 12\}$
2) $\{1, 2, 3, 5, 7, 8, 9, 11, 12\}$
3) $\{2, 4, 5, 7, 9, 11\}$
4) $\{2\}$
5) $\{\ \}$ *(empty set)*
6) $\{5, 7\}$
7) $\{1, 2, 3, 4, 5, 7, 8, 9, 11, 12\}$
8) $\{5, 7\}$
9) $\{\ \}$ *(empty set)*
10) $\{2\}$

Day 3: Algebraic Expressions

Topics that you'll learn today:

- ✓ Evaluating Expressions
- ✓ Simplifying Algebraic Expressions

"Do not worry about your difficulties in mathematics. I can assure you mine are still greater."

- Albert Einstein

Evaluating Expressions

Step-by-step guide:

✓ To evaluate an algebraic expression, substitute a number for each variable and perform the arithmetic operations.

Examples:

2) **Solve this expression.** $4(2a - b), a = 2, b = -1$

First substitute 2 for a, and -1 for b, then:

$4(2a - b), 8a - 4b = 8(2) - 4(-1) = 16 + 4 = 20$

3) **Solve this expression.** $2x + 6y, x = 1, y = 2$

First substitute 1 for x, and 2 for y, then:

$2x + 6y = 2(1) + 6(2) = 2 + 12 = 14$

✎ *Evaluate each expression using the values given.*

1) $x + 2y$,
   $x = 1, y = 2$

2) $2x - 3y$,
   $x = 1, y = -2$

3) $-a + 5b$,
   $a = -2, b = 3$

4) $-3a + 5b$,
   $a = 5, b = 2$

5) $5x + 8 - 3y$,
   $x = 5, y = 4$

6) $3x + 5y$,
   $x = 2, y = 3$

7) $7x + 6y$,
   $x = 2, y = 4$

8) $3a - (12 - b)$,
   $a = 3, b = 5$

9) $4z + 20 + 7k$,
   $z = -4, k = 5$

10) $xy + 15 + 4x$,
    $x = 6, y = 3$

11) $8x + 3 - 5y + 4$,
    $x = 6, y = 3$

12) $5 + 2(-3x - 4y)$,
    $x = 6, y = 5$

Simplifying Algebraic Expressions

Step-by-step guide:

- In algebra, a variable is a letter used to stand for a number. The most common letters are: $x, y, z, a, b, c, m, and\ n$.
- algebraic expression is an expression contains integers, variables, and the math operations such as addition, subtraction, multiplication, division, etc.
- In an expression, we can combine "like" terms. (values with same variable and same power)

Examples:

1) Simplify this expression. $(2x + 3x + 4) = ?$
   Combine like terms. Then: $(2x + 3x + 4) = 5x + 4$ (remember you cannot combine variables and numbers.
2) Simplify this expression. $12 - 3x^2 + 5x + 4x^2 = ?$
   Combine "like" terms: $-3x^2 + 4x^2 = x^2$
   Then: $= 12 + x^2 + 5x$. Write in standard form (biggest powers first): $x^2 + 5x + 12$

✍ *Simplify each expression.*

1) $x - 4 + 6 - 2x =$

2) $3 - 4x + 14 - 3x =$

3) $33x - 5 + 13 + 4x =$

4) $-3 - x^2 - 7x^2 =$

5) $4 + 11x^2 + 3 =$

6) $7x^2 + 5x + 6x^2 =$

7) $42x + 15 + 3x^2 =$

8) $6x(x - 2) - 5 =$

9) $7x - 6 + 9x + 3x^2 =$

10) $(-5)(7x - 2) + 12x =$

11) $15x - 6(6 - 7x) =$

12) $25x + 6(7x + 2) + 14 =$

Answers – Day 3

Evaluating Expressions

1) 5
2) 8
3) 17
4) −5
5) 21
6) 21
7) 38
8) 2
9) 39
10) 57
11) 40
12) −71

Simplifying Algebraic Expressions

1) $-x + 2$
2) $-7x + 17$
3) $37x + 8$
4) $-8x^2 - 3$
5) $11x^2 + 7$
6) $13x^2 + 5x$
7) $3x^2 + 42x + 15$
8) $6x^2 - 12x - 5$
9) $3x^2 + 16x - 6$
10) $-23x + 10$
11) $57x - 36$
12) $67x + 26$

Day 4: Equations

Math Topics that you'll learn today:

- ✓ One–Step Equations
- ✓ Multi–Step Equations

"Life is a math equation. In order to gain the most, you have to know how to convert negatives into positives."

~ Anonymous

One–Step Equations

Step-by-step guide:

✓ The values of two expressions on both sides of an equation are equal. $ax + b = c$
✓ You only need to perform one Math operation in order to solve the one-step equations.
✓ To solve one-step equation, find the inverse (opposite) operation is being performed.
✓ The inverse operations are:
  - Addition and subtraction
  - Multiplication and division

Examples:

1) **Solve this equation.** $2x = 16, x = ?$
   Here, the operation is multiplication (variable x is multiplied by 3) and its inverse operation is division. To solve this equation, divide both sides of **equation by** 2:
   $$2x = 16 \rightarrow 2x \div 2 = 16 \div 2 \rightarrow x = 8$$

2) **Solve this equation.** $x + 12 = 0, x = ?$
   Here, the operation is addition and its inverse operation is subtraction. To solve this equation, subtract 12 from both sides of the **equation:** $x + 12 - 12 = 0 - 12$
   Then simplify: $x + 12 - 12 = 0 - 12 \rightarrow x = -12$

✎ *Solve each equation.*

1) $14 = -2 + x, x =$ ____

2) $x + 7 = 14, x =$ ____

3) $x - 3 = 15, x =$ ____

4) $6 = 14 + x, x =$ ____

5) $x - 4 = 5, x =$ ____

6) $3 - x = -11, x =$ ____

7) $x - 5 = -15, x =$ ____

8) $x - 14 = 14, x =$ ____

9) $x - 15 = -30, x =$ ____

10) $x - 12 = 34, x =$ ____

11) $9 - x = 5, x =$ ____

12) $x - 16 = 16, x =$ ____

Multi–Step Equations

Step-by-step guide:

- ✓ Combine "like" terms on one side.
- ✓ Bring variables to one side by adding or subtracting.
- ✓ Simplify using the inverse of addition or subtraction.
- ✓ Simplify further by using the inverse of multiplication or division.

Examples:

1) **Solve this equation.** $-(8-x) = 6$

   First use Distributive Property: $-(8-x) = -8 + x$

   Now solve by subtract 6 to both sides of the equation. $-8 + x = 6 \to -8 + x - 6 = 6 - 6$

   Now simplify: $-14 + x = 0 \to x = 14$

2) **Solve this equation.** $2x + 5 = 15 - x$

   First bring variables to one side by adding x to both sides.

   $2x + 5 = 15 - x \to 3x + 5 = 15$. Now, subtract 15 from both sides:

   $3x + 5 - 15 = 15 - 15 \to 3x - 10 = 0 \to 3x = 10$

   Now, divide both sides by 3: $3x = 10 \to 3x \div 3 = \frac{10}{3} \to x = \frac{10}{3}$

✎ **Solve each equation.**

1) $-(3 - x) = 7$

2) $3x - 15 = 12$

3) $3x - 3 = 9$

4) $3x - 15 = 6$

5) $-3(5 + x) = 3$

6) $-5(3 + x) = 5$

7) $24 = -(x - 7)$

8) $6(4 - 2x) = 30$

9) $18 - 4x = -9 - x$

10) $14 - 2x = 14 + x$

11) $30 + 15x = -6 + 3x$

12) $18 = (-4x) - 9 + 3$

Answers – Day 4

One–Step Equations

1) 16
2) 7
3) 18
4) −8
5) 9
6) 14
7) −10
8) 28
9) −15
10) 46
11) 4
12) 32

Multi–Step Equations

1) 10
2) 9
3) 4
4) 7
5) −6
6) −4
7) −17
8) $-\frac{1}{2}$
9) 9
10) 0
11) −3
12) −6

Day 5: Inequalities

Math Topics that you'll learn today:

- ✓ Graphing Single–Variable Inequalities
- ✓ One–Step Inequalities

"Sometimes the questions are complicated and the answers are simple." - Dr. Seuss

Graphing Single-Variable Inequalities

Step-by-step guide:

- ✓ Inequality is similar to equations and uses symbols for "less than" (<) and "greater than" (>).
- ✓ To solve inequalities, we need to isolate the variable. (like in equations)
- ✓ To graph an inequality, find the value of the inequality on the number line.
- ✓ For less than or greater than draw open circle on the value of the variable.
- ✓ If there is an equal sign too, then use filled circle.
- ✓ Draw a line to the right or to the left for greater or less than.

Examples:

1) **Draw a graph for** $x > 4$

Since, the variable is greater than 4, then we need to find 4 and draw an open circle above it. Then, draw a line to the right.

2) **Graph this inequality.** $x < 5$

✍ Draw a graph for each inequality.

1) $x > 2$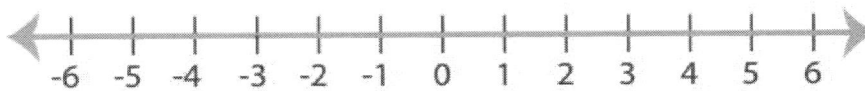

2) $x < -2$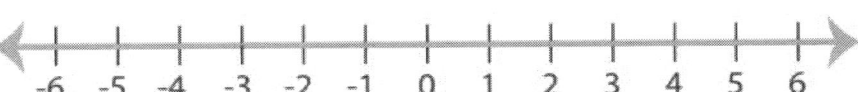

3) $x < 4$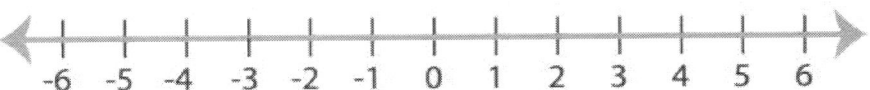

4) $x > -1$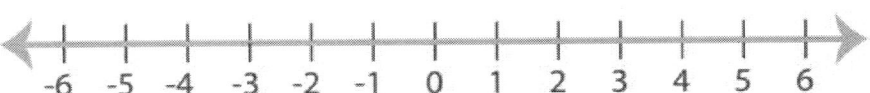

5) $x < 5$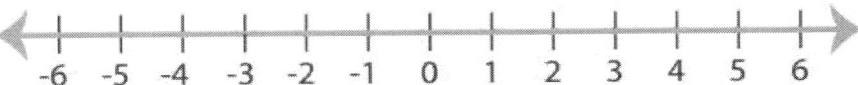

One–Step Inequalities

Step-by-step guide:

- ✓ Similar to equations, first isolate the variable by using inverse operation.
- ✓ For dividing or multiplying both sides by negative numbers, flip the direction of the inequality sign.

Examples:

1) **Solve and graph the inequality.** $x + 2 \geq 3$.

Subtract 2 from both sides. $x + 2 \geq 3 \rightarrow x + 2 - 2 \geq 3 - 2$, then: $x \geq 1$

2) **Solve this inequality.** $x - 1 \leq 2$

Add 1 to both sides. $x - 1 \leq 2 \rightarrow x - 1 + 1 \leq 2 + 1$, then: $x \leq 3$

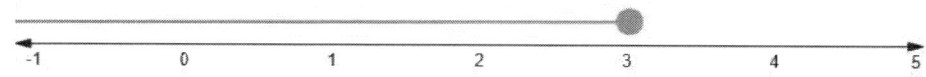

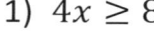 **Solve each inequality and graph it.**

1) $4x \geq 8$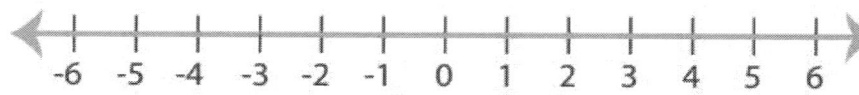

2) $2 + x \leq 6$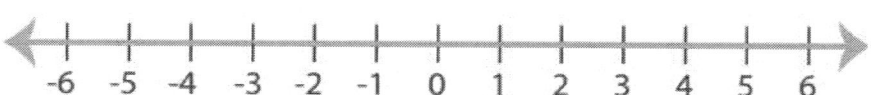

3) $x + 4 \leq 9$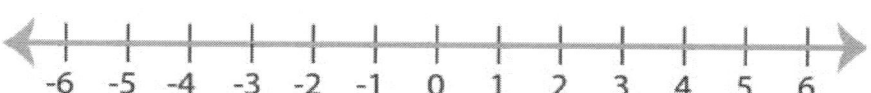

4) $8x \geq 24$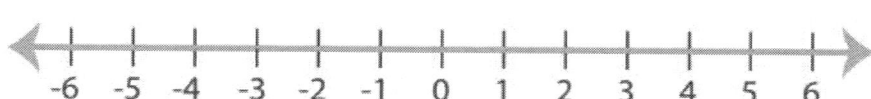

5) $5x \leq 20$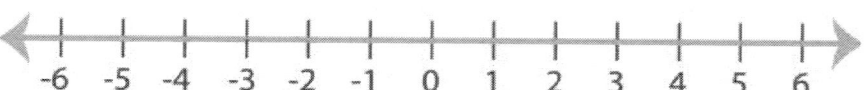

Answers – Day 5

Graphing Single–Variable Inequalities

1)

2)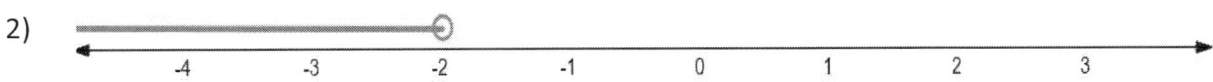

3)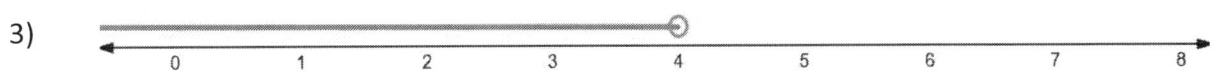

4)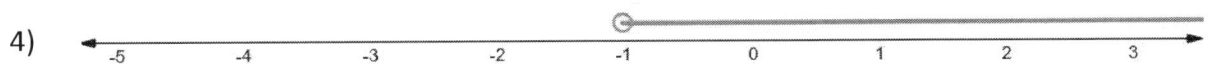

5)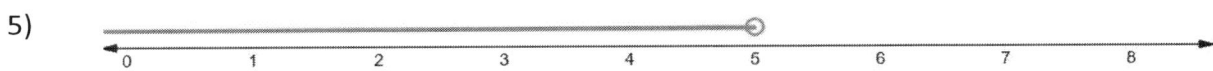

One–Step Inequalities

1)

2)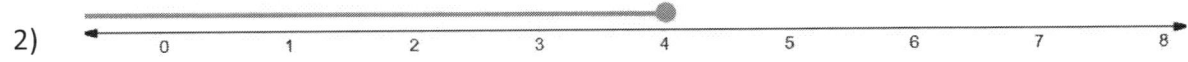

3)

4)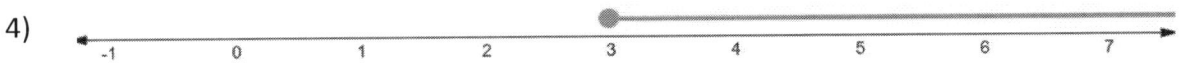

5)

Day 6: Multi–Step Inequalities

Math Topics that you'll learn today:

- ✓ Multi–Step Inequalities

Mathematics is the door and key to the sciences. ~ Roger Bacon

Multi-Step Inequalities

Step-by-step guide:

- ✓ Isolate the variable.
- ✓ Simplify using the inverse of addition or subtraction.
- ✓ Simplify further by using the inverse of multiplication or division.

Examples:

1) **Solve this inequality.** $x - 2 \leq 4$

   First add 2 to both sides: $x - 2 + 2 \leq 4 + 2 \to x \leq 6$

2) **Solve this inequality.** $2x + 6 \leq 10$

   First add 4 to both sides: $2x + 6 - 6 \leq 10 - 6$

   Then simplify: $2x + 6 - 6 \leq 10 - 6 \to 2x \leq 4$

   Now divide both sides by 2: $\frac{2x}{2} \leq \frac{4}{2} \to x \leq 2$

✎ *Solve each inequality.*

1) $x - 5 \leq 4$

2) $2x - 2 \leq 12$

3) $3 + 2x \leq 11$

4) $x - 6 \geq 12$

5) $3x - 6 \leq 12$

6) $7x - 3 \leq 18$

7) $2x - 3 < 23$

8) $15 - 2x \geq -15$

9) $7 + 3x < 25$

10) $2 + 4x \geq 18$

11) $7 + 3x < 34$

12) $5x - 2 < 8$

Answers – Day 6

Multi–Step inequalities

1) $x \leq 9$
2) $x \leq 7$
3) $x \leq 4$
4) $x \geq 18$
5) $x \leq 6$
6) $x \leq 3$

7) $x < 13$
8) $x \leq 15$
9) $x < 6$
10) $x \geq 4$
11) $x < 9$
12) $x < 2$

Day 7: System of Equations

Topics that you'll learn today:

- ✓ Solving Systems of Equations
- ✓ Systems of Equations Word Problems

"Do not worry about your difficulties in mathematics. I can assure you mine are still greater." – Albert Einstein

Systems of Equations

Step-by-step guide:

- A system of equations contains two equations and two variables. For example, consider the system of equations: $x - y = 1, x + y = 5$
- The easiest way to solve a system of equation is using the elimination method. The elimination method uses the addition property of equality. You can add the same value to each side of an equation.
- For the first equation above, you can add $x + y$ to the left side and 5 to the right side of the first equation: $x - y + (x + y) = 1 + 5$. Now, if you simplify, you get: $x - y + (x + y) = 1 + 5 \to 2x = 6 \to x = 3$. Now, substitute 3 for the x in the first equation: $3 - y = 1$. By solving this equation, $y = 2$

Example:

What is the value of $x + y$ in this system of equations? $\begin{cases} 2x + 5y = 11 \\ 4x - 2y = -26 \end{cases}$

Solving Systems of Equations by Elimination

Multiply the first equation by (-2), then add it to the second equation.

$\begin{matrix} -2(2x + 5y = 11) \\ 4x - 2y = -26 \end{matrix} \Rightarrow \begin{matrix} -4x - 10y = -22 \\ 4x - 2y = -26 \end{matrix} \Rightarrow -12y = -48 \Rightarrow y = 4$

Plug in the value of y into one of the equations and solve for x.

$2x + 5(4) = 11 \Rightarrow 2x + 20 = 11 \Rightarrow 2x = -9 \Rightarrow x = -4.5$

Thus, $x + y = -4.5 + 4 = -0.5$

✎ *Solve each system of equations.*

1) $-4x - 6y = 7$ $x = $ ___   2) $-5x + y = -3$ $x = $ ___

    $x - 2y = 7$ $y = $ ___ $3x - 7y = 21$ $y = $ ___

3) $3y = -6x + 12$ $x = $ ___   4) $x + 15y = 50$ $x = $ ___

    $8x - 9y = -10$ $y = $ ___ $x + 10y = 40$ $y = $ ___

5) $3x - 2y = 15$ $x = $ ___   6) $3x - 6y = -12$ $x = $ ___

    $3x - 5y = 15$ $y = $ ___ $-x - 3y = -6$ $y = $ ___

Systems of Equations Word Problems

Step-by-step guide:

✓ Define your variables, write two equations, and use elimination method for solving systems of equations.

Example:

Tickets to a movie cost $8 for adults and $5 for students. A group of friends purchased **20** tickets for $115.00. How many adults ticket did they buy? ____

Let x be the number of adult tickets and y be the number of student tickets. There are 20 tickets. Then: $x + y = 20$. The cost of adults' tickets is $8 and for students it is $5, and the total cost is $115. So, $8x + 5y = 115$. Now, we have a system of equations: $\begin{cases} x + y = 20 \\ 8x + 5y = 115 \end{cases}$

Multiply the first equation by -5 and add to the second equation: $-5(x + y = 20) = -5x - 5y = -100$

$8x + 5y + (-5x - 5y) = 115 - 100 \to 3x = 15 \to x = 5 \to 5 + y = 20 \to y = 15$. There are 5 adult tickets and 15 student tickets.

✍ Solve each word problem.

1) A theater is selling tickets for a performance. Mr. Smith purchased 8 senior tickets and 5 child tickets for $136 for his friends and family. Mr. Jackson purchased 4 senior tickets and 6 child tickets for $96. What is the price of a senior ticket? $_____

2) The difference of two numbers is 6. Their sum is 14. What is the bigger number? $_____

3) The sum of the digits of a certain two-digit number is 7. Reversing its digits increase the number by 9. What is the number? _____

4) The difference of two numbers is 18. Their sum is 66. What are the numbers?
_____

Answers – Day 7

Systems of Equations

1) $x = 2, y = -\frac{5}{2}$
2) $x = 0, y = -3$
3) $x = 1, y = 2$
4) $x = 20, y = 2$
5) $x = 5, y = 0$
6) $x = 0, y = 2$

Systems of Equations Word Problems

1) $12
2) 10
3) 34
4) 42, 24

Day 8:
Quadratic

Topics that you'll learn today:

✓ Solve a Quadratic Equation

✓ Graphing Quadratic Functions in Vertex Form

Mathematics is no more computation than typing is literature.

- John Allen Paulos

Solving a Quadratic Equation

Step-by-step guide:

- ✓ Write the equation in the form of: $ax^2 + bx + c = 0$
- ✓ Factorize the quadratic and solve for the variable.
- ✓ Use quadratic formula if you couldn't factorize the quadratic.
- ✓ Quadratic formula: $x = \frac{-b \pm \sqrt{b^2 - 4ac}}{2a}$

Examples:

Find the solutions of each quadratic.

1) $x^2 + 7x + 10 = 0$

Use quadratic formula: $= \frac{-b \pm \sqrt{b^2 - 4ac}}{2a}$, $a = 1, b = 7$ and $c = 10$

$x = \frac{-7 \pm \sqrt{7^2 - 4.1.10}}{2.1}$, $x_1 = \frac{-7 + \sqrt{7^2 - 4.1.10}}{2.1} = -2$, $x_2 = \frac{-7 - \sqrt{7^2 - 4.1.10}}{2.1} = -5$

2) $x^2 + 4x + 3 = 0$

Use quadratic formula: $= \frac{-b \pm \sqrt{b^2 - 4ac}}{2a}$, $a = 1, b = 4$ and $c = 3$

then: $x = \frac{-4 \pm \sqrt{4^2 - 4.1(3)}}{2(1)}$, $x_1 = \frac{-4 + \sqrt{4^2 - 4.1(3)}}{2(1)} = -1$, $x_2 = \frac{-4 - \sqrt{4^2 - 4.1(3)}}{2(1)} = -3$

✎ Solve each equation.

1) $x^2 - 5x - 14 = 0$

2) $x^2 + 8x + 15 = 0$

3) $x^2 - 5x - 36 = 0$

4) $x^2 - 12x - 35 = 0$

5) $x^2 + 12x + 32 = 0$

6) $5x^2 + 27x + 28 = 0$

7) $8x^2 + 26x + 15 = 0$

8) $3x^2 + 10x + 8 = 0$

9) $12x^2 + 30x + 12 = 0$

10) $9x^2 + 57x + 18 = 0$

Graphing Quadratic Functions

Step-by-step guide:

- ✓ Quadratic functions in vertex form: $y = a(x - h)^2 + k$ where (h, k) is the vertex of the function. The axis of symmetry is $x = h$
- ✓ Quadratic functions in standard form: $y = ax^2 + bx + c$ where $x = -\frac{b}{2a}$ is the value of x in the vertex of the function.
- ✓ To graph a quadratic function, first find the vertex, then substitute some values for x and solve for y.

Example:

Sketch the graph of $y = (x + 1)^2 - 2$.

The vertex of $y = (x + 1)^2 - 2$ is $(-1, -2)$. Substitute zero for x and solve for y. $y = (0 + 1)^2 - 2 = -1$. The y Intercept is $(0, -1)$.

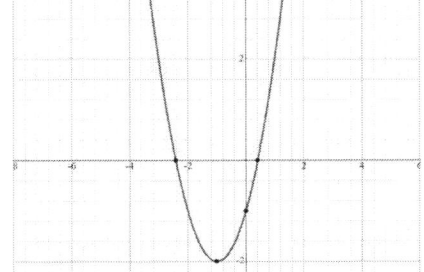

Now, you can simply graph the quadratic function.

✎ Sketch the graph of each function. Identify the vertex and axis of symmetry.

1) $y = 3(x - 5)^2 - 2$

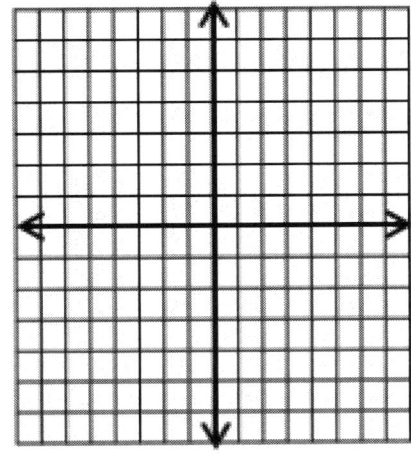

2) $y = x^2 - 3x + 15$

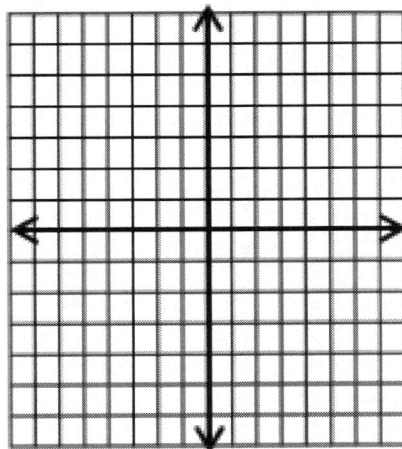

Answers – Day 8

Solving a Quadratic Equation

1) $x = -2, x = 7$
2) $x = -3, x = -5$
3) $x = 9, x = -4$
4) $x = 7, x = 5$
5) $x = -4, x = -8$
6) $x = -\frac{7}{5}, x = -4$
7) $x = -\frac{5}{2}, x = -\frac{3}{4}$
8) $x = -\frac{4}{3}, x = -2$
9) $x = -\frac{1}{2}, x = -2$
10) $x = -\frac{1}{3}, x = -6$

Graphing quadratic functions in vertex form

1)

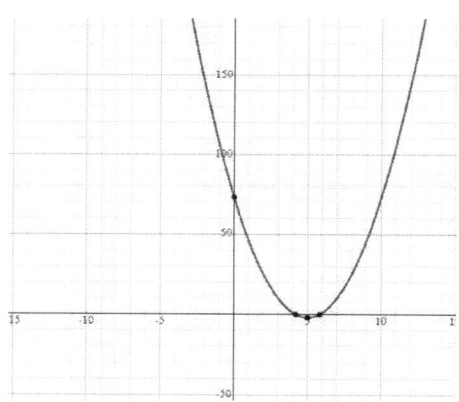

2)

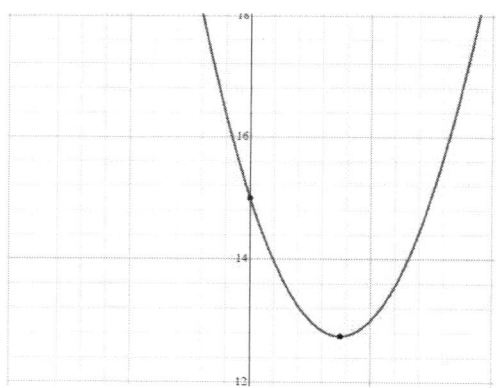

Day 9: Quadratic Inequalities

Topics that you'll learn today:

✓ Solve Quadratic Inequalities

✓ Graphing Quadratic Inequalities

Mathematics is on the artistic side a creation of new rhythms, orders, designs, harmonies, and on the knowledge side, is a systematic study of various rhythms, orders. - William L. Schaaf

Solving Quadratic Inequalities

Step-by-step guide:

- ✓ A quadratic inequality is one that can be written in one of the following standard forms:

  $ax^2 + bx + c > 0, ax^2 + bx + c < 0, ax^2 + bx + c \geq 0, ax^2 + bx + c \leq 0$

- ✓ Solving a quadratic inequality is like solving equations. We need to find the solutions.

Examples:

1) **Solve quadratic inequality.** $x^2 - 6x + 8 > 0$

   Factor: $x^2 - 6x + 8 > 0 \rightarrow (x-2)(x-4) > 0$

   Then the solution could be $x < 2$ or $x > 4$.

2) **Solve quadratic inequality.** $x^2 - 7x + 10 \geq 0$

   Factor: $x^2 - 7x + 10 \geq 0 \rightarrow (x-2)(x-5) \geq 0$. 2 and 5 are the solutions. Now, the solution could be $x < 2$ or $x = 2$ and $x = 5$ or $x > 5$.

✎ *Solve each quadratic inequality.*

1) $x^2 + 7x + 10 < 0$

2) $x^2 + 9x + 20 > 0$

3) $x^2 - 8x + 16 > 0$

4) $x^2 - 8x + 12 \leq 0$

5) $x^2 - 11x + 30 \leq 0$

6) $x^2 - 12x + 27 \geq 0$

7) $x^2 - 16x + 64 \geq 0$

8) $x^2 - 36 \leq 0$

9) $x^2 - 13x + 36 \geq 0$

10) $x^2 + 15x + 36 \leq 0$

11) $4x^2 - 6x - 9 > x^2$

12) $5x^2 - 15x + 10 < 0$

Graphing Quadratic inequalities

Step-by-step guide:

- ✓ A quadratic inequality is in the form $y > ax^2 + bx + c$ (or substitute $<, \leq,$ or $\geq$ for $>$).
- ✓ To graph a quadratic inequality, start by graphing the quadratic parabola. Then fill in the region either inside or outside of it, depending on the inequality.
- ✓ Choose a testing point and check the solution section.

Example: *Sketch the graph of $y > 3x^2$.*

First, graph $y = 3x^2$

Since, the inequality sing is $>$, we need to use dash lines.

Now, choose a testing point inside the parabola. Let's choose $(0,2)$. $y > 3x^2 \to 2 > 3(0)^2 \to 3 > 0$

This is true. So, inside the parabola is the solution section.

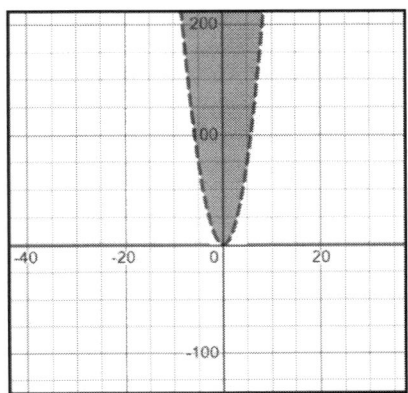

✎ Sketch the graph of each function.

1) $y < -2x^2$

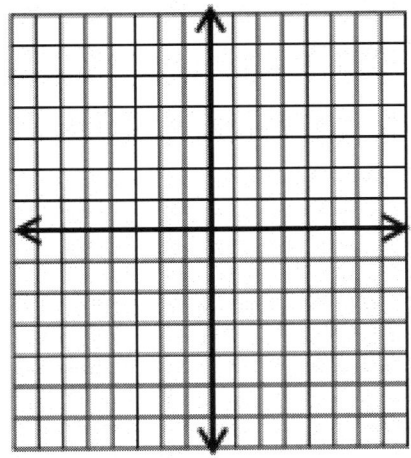

2) $y \geq 4x^2$

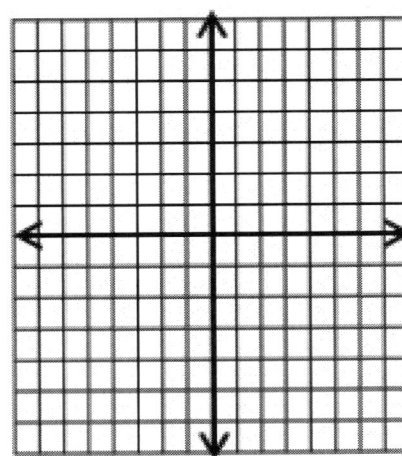

Answers – Day 9

Solve quadratic inequalities

1) $-5 < x < -2$
2) $x < -5 \text{ or } x > -4$
3) $x < 4 \text{ or } x > 4$
4) $2 \leq x \leq 6$
5) $5 \leq x \leq 6$
6) $x \leq 3 \text{ or } x \geq 9$
7) all real numbers
8) $-6 \leq x \leq 6$
9) $x \leq 4 \text{ or } x \geq 9$
10) $-12 \leq x \leq -3$
11) $x < -1 \text{ or } x > 3$
12) $1 < x < 2$

Graphing quadratic inequalities

1)
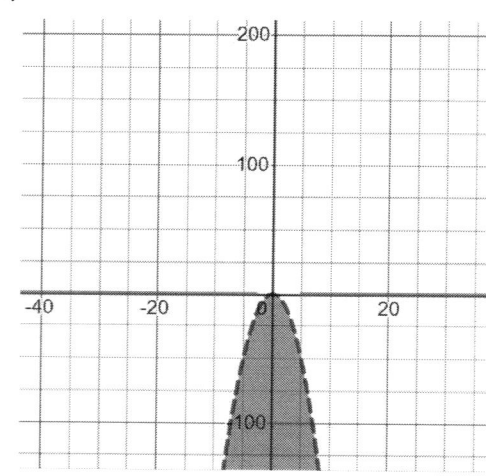

2)
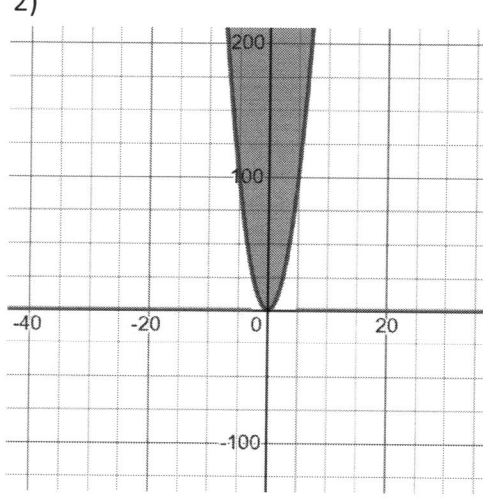

Day 10: Complex Numbers

Math Topics that you'll learn today:

- ✓ Adding and Subtracting Complex Numbers
- ✓ Multiplying and Dividing Complex Numbers

Mathematics is a hard thing to love. It has the unfortunate habit, like a rude dog, of turning its most unfavorable side towards you when you first make contact with it. – David Whiteland

Adding and Subtracting Complex Numbers

Step-by-step guide:

- ✓ A complex number is expressed in the form $a + bi$, where a and b are real numbers, and i, which is called an imaginary number, is a solution of the equation $x^2 = -1$
- ✓ For adding complex numbers: $(a + bi) + (c + di) = (a + c) + (b + d)i$
- ✓ For subtracting complex numbers: $(a + bi) - (c + di) = (a - c) + (b - d)i$

Examples:

1) Solve: $10 + (-5 - 3i) - 2$

   Remove parentheses: $10 + (-5 - 3i) - 2 \rightarrow 10 - 5 - 3i - 2$

   Combine like terms: $10 - 5 - 3i - 2 = 3 - 3i$

2) Solve: $-3 + (4i) + (9 - 2i)$

   Remove parentheses: $-3 + (4i) + (9 - 2i) \rightarrow -3 + 4i + 9 - 2i$

   Group like terms: $-3 + 4i + 9 - 2i \rightarrow 6 + 2i$

✍ Simplify.

1) $(1 - 2i) + (-4i) =$

2) $12 + (2 - 6i) =$

3) $-5 + (-2 - 8i) =$

4) $(-4i) - (7 - 2i) =$

5) $(-3 - 2i) - (2i) =$

6) $(8 - 6i) + (-5i) =$

7) $(-3 + 6i) - (-9 - i) =$

8) $(-5 + 15i) - (-3 + 3i) =$

9) $(-14 + i) - (-12 - 11i) =$

10) $(-18 - 3i) + (11 + 5i) =$

11) $(-11 - 9i) - (-9 - 3i) =$

12) $-8 + (2i) + (-8 + 6i) =$

Ace the CLEP College Algebra in 30 Days

Multiplying and Dividing Complex Numbers

Step-by-step guide:

- ✓ Multiplying complex numbers: $(a + bi) + (c + di) = (ac - bd) + (ad + bc)i$
- ✓ Dividing complex numbers: $\frac{a+bi}{c+di} = \frac{a+bi}{c+di} \times \frac{c-di}{c-di} = \frac{ac+bd}{c^2-d^2} + \frac{bc+ad}{c^2-d^2}i$
- ✓ Imaginary number rule: $i^2 = -1$

Examples:

1) Solve: $\frac{4-2i}{2+i} =$

   Use the rule for dividing complex numbers:
   $$\frac{a+bi}{c+di} = \frac{a+bi}{c+di} \times \frac{c-di}{c-di} = \frac{ac+bd}{c^2-d^2} + \frac{bc+ad}{c^2-d^2}i \rightarrow$$
   $$\frac{4-2i}{2+i} \times \frac{2-i}{2-i} = \frac{(4 \times (2)+(-2)(1)}{2^2+(1)^2} + \frac{(-2 \times (2) - (4)(1)}{2^2+(1)^2}i = \frac{6-8i}{5} = \frac{6}{5} - \frac{8}{5}i$$

2) Solve: $(2-3i)(4-3i)$

   Use the rule: $(a + bi) + (c + di) = (ac - bd) + (ad + bc)i$

   $(2.4 - (-3)(-3)) + (2(-3) + (-3).4)i = -1 - 18i$

✎ Simplify.

1) $(-2 - i)(4 + i) =$

2) $(2 - 2i)^2 =$

3) $(4 - 3i)(6 - 6i) =$

4) $(5 + 4i)^2 =$

5) $(4i)(-i)(2 - 5i) =$

6) $(2 - 8i)(3 - 5i) =$

7) $\frac{9i}{3-i} =$

8) $\frac{2+4i}{14+4i} =$

9) $\frac{5+6i}{-1+8i} =$

10) $\frac{-8-i}{-4-6i} =$

11) $\frac{-1+5i}{-8-7i} =$

12) $\frac{-2-9i}{-2+7i} =$

Answers – Day 10

Adding and subtracting complex numbers

1) $1 - 6i$
2) $14 - 6i$
3) $-7 - 8i$
4) $-7 - 2i$
5) $-3 - 4i$
6) $8 - 11i$
7) $6 + 7i$
8) $-2 + 12i$
9) $-2 + 12i$
10) $-7 + 2i$
11) $-2 - 6i$
12) $-16 + 8i$

Multiplying and dividing complex numbers

1) $-7 - 6i$
2) $-8i$
3) $6 - 42i$
4) $9 + 40i$
5) $8 - 20i$
6) $-34 - 34i$
7) $-\frac{9}{10} + \frac{27}{10}i$
8) $\frac{11}{53} + \frac{12}{53}i$
9) $\frac{43}{65} - \frac{46}{65}i$
10) $\frac{19}{26} + \frac{11}{13}i$
11) $-\frac{27}{113} - \frac{47}{113}i$
12) $-\frac{59}{53} + \frac{32}{53}i$

Day 11: Imaginary Numbers and Polynomials

Math Topics that you'll learn today:

✓ Rationalizing Imaginary Denominators

✓ Writing Polynomials in Standard Form

"Nature is written in mathematical language." - Galileo Galilei

Rationalizing Imaginary Denominators

Step-by-step guide:

- Step 1: Find the conjugate (it's the denominator with different sign between the two terms.
- Step 2: Multiply numerator and denominator by the conjugate.
- Step 3: Simplify if needed.

Examples:

1) Solve: $\dfrac{2-3i}{6i}$

   Multiply by the conjugate: $\dfrac{-i}{-i} \cdot \dfrac{2-3i}{6i} = \dfrac{(2-3i)(-i)}{6i(-i)} = \dfrac{-3-2i}{6} = -\dfrac{1}{2} - \dfrac{1}{3}i$

2) Solve: $\dfrac{8i}{2-4i}$

   Factor $2 - 4i = 2(1 - 2i)$, then: $\dfrac{8i}{2(1-2i)} = \dfrac{4i}{(1-2i)}$

   Multiply by the conjugate $\dfrac{1+2i}{1+2i}$: $\dfrac{4i(1+2i)}{(1-2i)(1+2i)} = \dfrac{-8+4i}{5} = -\dfrac{8}{5} + \dfrac{4}{5}i$

✎ Simplify.

1) $\dfrac{-8}{-5i} =$

2) $\dfrac{-5}{-i} =$

3) $\dfrac{3}{5i} =$

4) $\dfrac{6}{-4i} =$

5) $\dfrac{-6-i}{-1+6i} =$

6) $\dfrac{-9-3i}{-3+3i} =$

7) $\dfrac{4i+1}{-1+3i} =$

8) $\dfrac{6-3i}{2-i} =$

9) $\dfrac{-5+2i}{2-3i} =$

10) $\dfrac{-9-i}{2-i} =$

11) $\dfrac{-10-5i}{-6+6i} =$

12) $\dfrac{-5-9i}{9+8i} =$

Writing Polynomials in Standard Form

Step-by-step guide:

- ✓ A polynomial function $f(x)$ of degree n is of the form
$$f(x) = a_n x^n + a_{n-1} x_{n-1} + \cdots + a_1 x + a_0$$
- ✓ The first term is the one with the biggest power!

Example:

1) Write this polynomial in standard form. $8 + 5x^2 - 3x^3 =$

   The first term is the one with the biggest power: $8 + 5x^2 - 3x^3 = -3x^3 + 5x^2 + 8$

2) Write this polynomial in standard form. $5x^2 - 9x^5 + 8x^3 - 11 =$

   The first term is the one with the biggest power: $5x^2 - 9x^5 + 8x^3 - 11 = -9x^5 + 8x^3 + 5x^2 - 11$

✎ *Write each polynomial in standard form.*

1) $2x - 5x =$

2) $5 + 12x - 8x =$

3) $x^2 - 2x^3 + 1 =$

4) $2 + 2x^2 - 1 =$

5) $-x^2 + 4x - 2x^3 =$

6) $-2x^2 + 2x^3 + 12 =$

7) $18 - 5x + 9x^4 =$

8) $2x^2 + 13x - 2x^3 =$

9) $8 + 4x^2 - x^3 =$

10) $2x + 3x^3 - 2x^2 =$

11) $-4x^2 + 4x - 6x^3 =$

12) $-3x^2 + 2 - 5x =$

Answers – Day 11

Rationalizing imaginary denominators

1) $\frac{-8}{5}i$
2) $-5i$
3) $-\frac{3}{5}i$
4) $\frac{3}{2}i$
5) i
6) $1 + 2i$
7) $\frac{11}{10} - \frac{7}{10}i$
8) 3
9) $-\frac{16}{13} - \frac{11}{13}i$
10) $-\frac{17}{5} + \frac{11}{5}i$
11) $\frac{5}{12} + \frac{5}{4}i$
12) $-\frac{117}{145} - \frac{41}{145}i$

Writing Polynomials in Standard Form

1) $-3x$
2) $4x + 5$
3) $-2x^3 + x^2 + 1$
4) $2x^2 + 1$
5) $-2x^3 - x^2 + 4x$
6) $2x^3 - 2x^2 + 12$
7) $9x^4 - 5x + 18$
8) $-2x^3 + 2x^2 + 13x$
9) $-x^3 + 4x^2 + 8$
10) $3x^3 - 2x^2 + 2x$
11) $-6x^3 - 4x^2 + 4x$
12) $-3x^2 - 5x + 2$

Day 12: Adding and Subtracting Polynomials

Math Topics that you'll learn today:

- ✓ Simplifying Polynomials

- ✓ Adding and Subtracting Polynomials

Mathematics is the supreme judge; from its decisions there is no appeal. –Tobias Dantzig

Simplifying Polynomials

Step-by-step guide:

- ✓ Find "like" terms. (they have same variables with same power).
- ✓ Use "FOIL". (First-Out-In-Last) for binomials:
$$(x + a)(x + b) = x^2 + (b + a)x + ab$$
- ✓ Add or Subtract "like" terms using order of operation.

Example:

1) Simplify this expression. $2x(2x - 4) =$

   Use Distributive Property: $2x(2x - 4) = 4x^2 - 8x$

2) Simplify this expression. $(x + 2)(x - 5) =$

   First apply FOIL method: $(a + b)(c + d) = ac + ad + bc + bd$

   $(x + 2)(x - 5) = x^2 - 5x + 2x - 10$

   Now combine like terms: $x^2 - 5x + 2x - 10 = x^2 - 3x - 10$

✎ *Simplify each expression.*

1) $2(4x - 6) =$

2) $5(3x - 4) =$

3) $x(2x - 5) =$

4) $4(5x + 3) =$

5) $2x(6x - 2) =$

6) $x(3x + 8) =$

7) $(x - 2)(x + 4) =$

8) $(x + 3)(x + 2) =$

9) $(x - 4)(x - 7) =$

10) $(2x + 4)(2x - 5) =$

11) $(4x - 3)(x - 6) =$

12) $(3x + 5)(2x + 4) =$

Adding and Subtracting Polynomials

Step-by-step guide:

- ✓ Adding polynomials is just a matter of combining like terms, with some order of operations considerations thrown in.
- ✓ Be careful with the minus signs, and don't confuse addition and multiplication!

Example:

1) **Simplify the expressions.** $(2x^3 - 4x^4) - (2x^4 - 6x^3) =$

   First use Distributive Property for $-(2x^4 - 6x^3) = -2x^4 + 6x^3$

   $(2x^3 - 4x^4) - (2x^4 - 6x^3) = 2x^3 - 4x^4 - 2x^4 + 6x^3$

   Now combine like terms: $2x^3 - 4x^4 - 2x^4 + 6x^3 = -6x^4 + 8x^3$

2) **Add expressions.** $(x^3 - 2) + (5x^3 - 3x^2) =$

   Remove parentheses: $(x^3 - 2) + (5x^3 - 3x^2) = x^3 - 2 + 5x^3 - 3x^2$

   Now combine like terms: $x^3 - 2 + 5x^3 - 3x^2 = 6x^3 - 3x^2 - 2$

✍ *Add or subtract expressions.*

1) $(x^2 - x) + (3x^2 - 5x) =$

2) $(x^3 + 2x) - (3x^3 + 2) =$

3) $(2x^3 - 4) + (2x^3 - 2) =$

4) $(-x^2 - 2) + (2x^2 + 1) =$

5) $(4x^2 + 3) - (3 - 3x^2) =$

6) $(x^3 + 3x^2) - (x^3 - 8) =$

7) $(7x - 9) + (3x + 5) =$

8) $(x^4 - 2x) - (x - x^4) =$

9) $(2x - 4x^3) - (2x^3 + 3x) =$

10) $(x^3 + 5) - (5 - 2x^3) =$

11) $(3x^2 + 2x^3) - (4x^3 + 5) =$

12) $(6x^2 - x) + (2x - 5x^2) =$

Answers – Day 12

Simplifying Polynomials

1) $8x - 12$
2) $15x - 20$
3) $2x^2 - 5x$
4) $20x + 12$
5) $12x^2 - 4x$
6) $3x^2 + 8x$
7) $x^2 + 2x - 8$
8) $x^2 + 5x + 6$
9) $x^2 - 11x + 28$
10) $4x^2 - 2x - 20$
11) $4x^2 - 27x + 18$
12) $6x^2 + 22x + 20$

Adding and Subtracting Polynomials

1) $4x^2 - 6x$
2) $-2x^3 + 2x - 2$
3) $4x^3 - 6$
4) $x^2 - 1$
5) $7x^2$
6) $3x^2 + 8$
7) $10x - 4$
8) $2x^4 - 3x$
9) $-6x^3 - 3x$
10) $3x^3$
11) $-2x^3 + 3x^2 - 5$
12) $x^2 + x$

Day 13: Multiplying and Dividing Monomials

Math Topics that you'll learn today:

- ✓ Multiplying Monomials
- ✓ Multiplying and Dividing Monomials

Mathematics is the supreme judge; from its decisions there is no appeal. – Tobias Dantzig

Multiplying Monomials

Step-by-step guide:

✓ A monomial is a polynomial with just one term, like $2x$ or $7y$.

Example:

1) **Multiply expressions.** $-2xy^4z^2 \times 4x^2y^5z^3 =$

   Use this formula: $x^a \times x^b = x^{a+b}$

   $x \times x^2 = x^{1+2} = x^3$, $y^4 \times y^5 = y^{4+5} = y^9$ and $z^2 \times z^3 = z^{2+3} = z^5$

   Then: $-2xy^4z^2 \times 4x^2y^5z^3 = -8x^3y^9z^5$

2) **Multiply expressions.** $-4a^4b^3 \times 5a^3b^2 =$

   Use this formula: $x^a \times x^b = x^{a+b}$

   $a^4 \times a^3 = a^{4+3} = a^7$ and $b^3 \times b^2 = b^{3+2} = b^5$

   Then: $-4a^4b^3 \times 5a^3b^2 = -20a^7b^5$

✎ *Simplify each expression.*

1) $(-2x^4) \times (-5x^3) =$

2) $8x^8 \times -2x^2 =$

3) $5xy^4 \times 2x^2 =$

4) $-2x^6y \times 8xy =$

5) $3x^5 \times (-4x^3y^5) =$

6) $9x^3y^2 \times 3x^2y =$

7) $7xy^4 \times 8x^3y^5 =$

8) $(-5x^2y^4) \times (-2xy^3) =$

9) $9x^5y^2 \times 5x^6y^3 =$

10) $12x^5y^2 \times 2x^3y^3 =$

11) $11x^4y^3z \times 3x^5z^2 =$

12) $20x^5y^8 \times 3x^2y^4 =$

Multiplying and Dividing Monomials

Step-by-step guide:

- ✓ When you divide two monomials you need to divide their coefficients and then divide their variables.
- ✓ In case of exponents with the same base, you need to subtract their powers.
- ✓ Exponent's rules:

$$x^a \times x^b = x^{a+b}, \qquad \frac{x^a}{x^b} = x^{a-b}$$
$$\frac{1}{x^b} = x^{-b}, \quad (x^a)^b = x^{a \times b}$$
$$(xy)^a = x^a \times y^a$$

Example:

1) **Multiply expressions.** $(8x^5)(-2x^4) =$
Use this formula: $x^a \times x^b = x^{a+b} \rightarrow x^5 \times x^4 = x^9$
Then: $(8x^5)(-2x^4) = -16x^9$

2) **Dividing expressions.** $\frac{-12x^4y^3}{2xy^2} =$
Use this formula: $\frac{x^a}{x^b} = x^{a-b}$, $\frac{x^4}{x} = x^{4-1} = x^3$ and $\frac{y^3}{y^2} = y$
Then: $\frac{-12x^4y^3}{2xy^2} = -6x^3y$

✎ *Simplify each expression.*

1) $(x^2y)(xy^2) =$

2) $(x^4y^2)(2x^5y) =$

3) $(-2x^2y)(4x^4y^3) =$

4) $(-3x^5y^2)(2x^2y^4) =$

5) $(-4x^5y^3)(-2x^3y^4) =$

6) $(6x^6y^5)(3x^3y^8) =$

7) $\frac{-2x^4y^3}{x^2y^2} =$

8) $\frac{8x^4y^7}{2x^3y^4} =$

9) $\frac{25x^6y^5}{5x^3y^2} =$

10) $\frac{18x^{12}y^{14}}{6x^8y^6} =$

11) $\frac{45x^{13}y^{15}}{9x^9y^4} =$

12) $\frac{-60x^{20}y^{16}}{3x^{11}y^{13}} =$

Answers – Day 13

Multiplying Monomials

1) $10x^7$
2) $-16x^{10}$
3) $10x^3y^4$
4) $-16x^7y^2$
5) $-12x^8y^5$
6) $27x^5y^3$
7) $56x^4y^9$
8) $10x^3y^7$
9) $45x^{11}y^5$
10) $24x^8y^5$
11) $33x^9y^3z^3$
12) $60x^7y^{12}$

Multiplying and Dividing Monomials

1) x^3y^3
2) $2x^9y^3$
3) $-8x^6y^4$
4) $-6x^7y^6$
5) $8x^8y^7$
6) $18x^9y^{13}$
7) $-2x^2y$
8) $4xy^3$
9) $5x^3y^3$
10) $3x^4y^8$
11) $5x^4y^{11}$
12) $-20x^9y^3$

Day 14: Monomials and Binomials

Math Topics that you'll learn today:

- ✓ Multiplying a Polynomial and a Monomial
- ✓ Multiplying Binomials

Mathematics is, I believe, the chief source of the belief in eternal and exact truth, as well as a sensible intelligible world. – Bertrand Russell

Multiplying a Polynomial and a Monomial

Step-by-step guide:

- ✓ When multiplying monomials, use the product rule for exponents.
- ✓ When multiplying a monomial by a polynomial, use the distributive property.
$$a \times (b + c) = a \times b + a \times c$$

Example:

1) **Multiply expressions.** $2x(-2x + 4) =$

   Use Distributive Property: $2x(-2x + 4) = -4x^2 + 8x$

2) **Multiply expressions.** $-2x(3x^2 + 4y^2) =$

   Use Distributive Property: $-2x(3x^2 + 4y^2) = -6x^3 - 8xy^2$

Find each product.

1) $-2x(5x + 2y) =$

2) $3x(2x - y) =$

3) $4x(x + 5y) =$

4) $-4x(6x - 3) =$

5) $x(-2x + 9y) =$

6) $2x(5x - 8y) =$

7) $x(2x + 4y - 3) =$

8) $2x(x^2 - 2y^2) =$

9) $-4x(2x + 4y) =$

10) $3(x^2 + 7y^2) =$

11) $4x(-x^2y + 2y) =$

12) $5(x^2 - 4xy + 6) =$

Multiplying Binomials

Step-by-step guide:

- Use "FOIL". (First-Out-In-Last)
$$(x + a)(x + b) = x^2 + (b + a)x + ab$$

Example:

1) **Multiply Binomials.** $(x + 3)(x - 2) =$

   Use "FOIL". (First–Out–In–Last): $(x + 3)(x - 2) = x^2 - 2x + 3x - 6$

   Then simplify: $x^2 - 2x + 3x - 6 = x^2 + x - 6$

2) **Multiply Binomials.** $(x - 4)(x - 2) =$

   Use "FOIL". (First–Out–In–Last):

   $(x - 4)(x - 2) = x^2 - 2x - 4x + 8$

   Then simplify: $x^2 - 6x + 8 =$

✎ *Find each product.*

1) $(x - 2)(x + 4) =$

2) $(x + 5)(x - 2) =$

3) $(x - 3)(x - 4) =$

4) $(x + 2)(x + 2) =$

5) $(x - 6)(x - 3) =$

6) $(x + 5)(x + 7) =$

7) $(x + 2)(x - 8) =$

8) $(x - 9)(x + 4) =$

9) $(x + 5)(x + 6) =$

10) $(x - 8)(x + 3) =$

11) $(x + 5)(x + 5) =$

12) $(x + 7)(x + 4) =$

Answers – Day 14

Multiplying a Polynomial and a Monomial

1) $-10x^2 - 4xy$
2) $6x^2 - 3xy$
3) $4x^2 + 20xy$
4) $-24x^2 + 12x$
5) $-2x^2 + 9xy$
6) $10x^2 - 16xy$
7) $2x^2 + 4xy - 3x$
8) $2x^3 - 4xy^2$
9) $-8x^2 - 16xy$
10) $3x^2 + 21y^2$
11) $-4x^3y + 8xy$
12) $5x^2 - 20xy + 30$

Multiplying Binomials

1) $x^2 + 2x - 8$
2) $x^2 + 3x - 10$
3) $x^2 - 7x + 12$
4) $x^2 + 4x + 4$
5) $x^2 - 9x + 18$
6) $x^2 + 12x + 35$
7) $x^2 - 6x - 16$
8) $x^2 - 5x - 36$
9) $x^2 + 11x + 30$
10) $x^2 - 5x - 24$
11) $x^2 + 10x + 25$
12) $x^2 + 11x + 28$

Day 15: Operations with Polynomials

Math Topics that you'll learn today:

- ✓ Factoring Trinomials
- ✓ Operations with Polynomials

Mathematics is a hard thing to love. It has the unfortunate habit, like a rude dog, of turning its most unfavorable side towards you when you first make contact with it. ~ David Whiteland

Factoring Trinomials

Step-by-step guide:

- ✓ "FOIL":
$$(x + a)(x + b) = x^2 + (b + a)x + ab$$
- ✓ "Difference of Squares":
$$a^2 - b^2 = (a + b)(a - b)$$
$$a^2 + 2ab + b^2 = (a + b)(a + b)$$
$$a^2 - 2ab + b^2 = (a - b)(a - b)$$
- ✓ "Reverse FOIL":
$$x^2 + (b + a)x + ab = (x + a)(x + b)$$

Example:

1) **Factor this trinomial.** $x^2 - 3x - 18 =$
Break the expression into groups: $(x^2 + 3x) + (-6x - 18)$
Now factor out x from $x^2 + 3x$: $x(x + 2)$, and factor out -6 from $-6x + 18$: $-6(x + 3)$
Then: $= x(x + 3) - 6(x + 3)$, now factor out like term: $x + 3$
Then: $(x + 3)(x - 6)$

2) **Factor this trinomial.** $x^2 + x - 20 =$
Break the expression into groups: $(x^2 - 4x) + (5x - 20)$
Now factor out x from $x^2 - 4x$: $x(x + 3)$, and factor out 5 from $6x - 18$: $5(x - 4)$
Then: $= x(x - 4) + 5(x - 4)$, now factor out like term: $x - 4$
Then: $(x + 5)(x - 4)$

✏ Factor each trinomial.

1) $x^2 + 3x - 10 =$

2) $x^2 - x - 6 =$

3) $x^2 + 8x + 15 =$

4) $x^2 - 7x + 12 =$

5) $x^2 - x - 20 =$

6) $x^2 + 11x + 18 =$

7) $x^2 + 3x - 28 =$

8) $x^2 - 2x - 48 =$

9) $x^2 - 13x + 36 =$

10) $x^2 - x - 56 =$

11) $x^2 - 4x - 45 =$

12) $x^2 - 8x - 48 =$

Operations with Polynomials

Step-by-step guide:

✓ When multiplying a monomial by a polynomial, use the distributive property.

$$a \times (b + c) = a \times b + a \times c$$

Example:

1) **Multiply.** $4(3x - 5) =$

Use the distributive property: $4(3x - 5) = 12x - 20$

2) **Multiply.** $6x(3x + 7) =$

Use the distributive property: $6x(3x + 7) = 18x^2 + 42x$

✏️ *Find each product.*

1) $2(3x + 2) =$

2) $-3(2x + 5) =$

3) $4(7x - 3) =$

4) $5(2x - 4) =$

5) $3x(2x - 7) =$

6) $x^2(3x + 4) =$

7) $x^3(x + 5) =$

8) $x^4(5x - 3) =$

9) $4(2x^2 + 3x - 2) =$

10) $-2(x^2 - 6x + 5) =$

11) $5(2x^2 + 4x - 6) =$

12) $-x(3x^2 + 7x + 5) =$

Answers – Day 15

Factoring Trinomials

1) $(x-2)(x+5)$
2) $(x+2)(x-3)$
3) $(x+5)(x+3)$
4) $(x-3)(x-4)$
5) $(x-5)(x+4)$
6) $(x+2)(x+9)$
7) $(x+7)(x-4)$
8) $(x-8)(x+6)$
9) $(x-4)(x-9)$
10) $(x-8)(x+7)$
11) $(x-9)(x+5)$
12) $(x+4)(x-12)$

Operations with Polynomials

1) $6x+4$
2) $-6x-15$
3) $28x-12$
4) $10x-20$
5) $6x^2-21x$
6) $3x^3+4x^2$
7) x^4+5x^3
8) $5x^5-3x^4$
9) $8x^2+12x-8$
10) $-2x^2+12x-10$
11) $10x^2+20x-30$
12) $-3x^3-7x^2-5x$

Day 16: Functions

Math Topics that you'll learn today:

- ✓ Function Notation
- ✓ Adding and Subtracting Functions

"The mathematician does not study pure mathematics because it is useful; he studies it because he delights in it and he delights in it because it is beautiful" Georg Cantor

Function Notation

Step-by-step guide:

✓ Functions are mathematical operations that assign unique outputs to given inputs.
✓ Function notation is the way a function is written. It is meant to be a precise way of giving information about the function without a rather lengthy written explanation.
✓ The most popular function notation is $f(x)$ which is read "f of x".

Examples:

1) Evaluate: $h(n) = n^2 - 2$, find $h(4)$. Substitute x with 4:

   Then: $h(n) = n^2 - 2 \rightarrow h(4) = (4)^2 - 2 \rightarrow h(4) = 16 - 2 \rightarrow h(4) = 14$

2) Evaluate: $w(x) = 4x - 1$, find $w(2)$. Substitute x with 4: Then: $w(x) = 4x - 1 \rightarrow w(2) = 4(2) - 1 \rightarrow w(2) = 8 - 1 \rightarrow w(2) = 7$

✍ **Evaluate each function.**

1) $f(x) = 2x + 8$, find $f(-1)$

2) $g(n) = n + 12$, find $g(2)$

3) $g(n) = -2n + 3$, find $g(-2)$

4) $h(n) = -2n^2 - 6n$, find $h(-1)$

5) $g(a) = 3a^2 + 2a$, find $g(3)$

6) $h(x) = x^2 + 1$, find $h(-2)$

7) $h(x) = x^3 + 8$, find $h(-1)$

8) $h(x) = 2x^2 - 10$, find $h(4)$

9) $h(a) = -2a - 5$, find $h(3)$

10) $k(a) = -7a + 3$, find $k(-2)$

11) $h(x) = 4x + 5$, find $h(6)$

12) $h(n) = -n^2 - 10$, find $h(5)$

Adding and Subtracting Functions

Step-by-step guide:

- ✓ Just like we can add and subtract numbers, we can add and subtract functions. For example, if we had functions f and g, we could create two new functions:
- ✓ f + g and f - g.

Examples:

1) $g(a) = a - 1$, $f(a) = a + 5$, Find: $(g + f)(-1)$

   $(g + f)(a) = g(a) + f(a)$, Then: $(g + f)(a) = a - 1 + a + 5 = 2a + 4$

   Substitute a with -1: $(g + f)(a) = 2a + 4 = 2(-1) + 4 = -2 + 4 = 2$

2) $f(x) = 3x - 3$, $g(x) = x - 5$, Find: $(f - g)(3)$

   $(f - g)(x) = f(x) - g(x)$, then: $(f - g)(x) = 3x - 3 - (x - 5) = 3x - 3 - x + 5$

   $$= 2x + 2$$

   Substitute x with 3: $(f - g)(1) = 2(3) + 2 = 8$

✍ *Perform the indicated operation.*

1) $g(x) = x + 2$
   $h(x) = 2x + 3$
   Find: $g(-1) - h(-1)$

2) $h(x) = 2x + 1$
   $g(x) = -x + 4$
   Find: $(h + g)(2)$

5) $g(x) = x^2 - 1$
   $f(x) = 2x + 12$
   Find: $(g - f)(2)$

3) $f(x) = 2x^2 - 1$
   $g(x) = x^2 + 2$
   Find: $(f - g)(-1)$

4) $h(n) = -n^2 + 3$
   $g(n) = -n + 9$
   Find: $(h - g)(3)$

6) $g(x) = 2x^3 + 8$
   $f(x) = -2x^2 - 10$
   Find: $(g + f)(2)$

Answers – Day 16

Function Notation

1) 6
2) 14
3) 7
4) 4
5) 33
6) 5
7) 7
8) 22
9) -11
10) -11
11) 29
12) -35

Adding and Subtracting Functions

1) 0
2) 7
3) -13
4) -2
5) -12
6) 6

Day 17: Multiplying and Dividing Functions

Math Topics that you'll learn today:

- ✓ Multiplying and Dividing Functions
- ✓ Composition of Functions

Mathematics is a hard thing to love. It has the unfortunate habit, like a rude dog, of turning its most unfavorable side towards you when you first make contact with it. ~ David Whiteland

Multiplying and Dividing Functions

Step-by-step guide:

✓ Just like we can multiply and divide numbers, we can multiply and divide functions. For example, if we had functions f and g, we could create two new functions: f × g, and $\frac{f}{g}$.

Examples:

1) $g(x) = x + 1, f(x) = x - 2$, Find: $(g.f)(2)$

   $(g.f)(x) = g(x).f(x) = (x+1)(x-2) = x^2 - 2x + x - 2 = x^2 - x - 2$

   Substitute x with 2:

   $(g.f)(x) = x^2 - x - 2 = (2)^2 - 2 - 2 = 4 - 2 - 2 = 0$

2) $f(x) = x - 2, h(x) = x + 8$, Find: $\left(\frac{f}{h}\right)(-1)$

   $\left(\frac{f}{h}\right)(x) = \frac{f(x)}{h(x)} = \frac{x-2}{x+8}$

   Substitute x with -1: $\left(\frac{f}{h}\right)(x) = \frac{x-2}{x+8} = \frac{(-1)-2}{(-1)+8} = \frac{-3}{7} = -\frac{3}{7}$

✎ *Perform the indicated operation.*

1) $f(x) = x - 1$
   $g(x) = x + 4$
   Find $\left(\frac{f}{g}\right)(2)$

2) $g(a) = 2a + 6$
   $f(a) = a - 12$
   Find $\left(\frac{g}{f}\right)(4)$

3) $g(x) = 2x + 4$
   $h(x) = x - 3$
   Find $(g.h)(-1)$

4) $g(n) = n^2 + 6$
   $h(n) = 2n - 8$
   Find $(g.h)(2)$

5) $f(x) = x^2 - 2$
   $g(x) = x + 1$
   Find $(f.g)(2)$

6) $f(x) = 2a^2 + 4$
   $g(x) = 6 + 2a$
   Find $\left(\frac{f}{g}\right)(2)$

Composition of Functions

Step-by-step guide:

- ✓ The term "composition of functions" (or "composite function") refers to the combining together of two or more functions in a manner where the output from one function becomes the input for the next function.
- ✓ The notation used for composition is: $(f \circ g)(x) = f(g(x))$

Examples:

1) **Using** $f(x) = x - 2$ **and** $g(x) = x$, **find:** $f(g(2))$

   $(f \circ g)(x) = f(g(x))$

   Then: $(f \circ g)(x) = f(g(x)) = f(x) = x - 2$

   Substitute x with 2: $(f \circ g)(2) = 2 - 2 = 0$

2) **Using** $f(x) = x + 8$ **and** $g(x) = x - 2$, **find:** $g(f(4))$

   $(f \circ g)(x) = f(g(x))$

   Then: $(g \circ f)(x) = g(f(x)) = g(x + 8)$, now substitute x in f(x) by $x + 8$. Then:
   $g(x + 8) = (x + 8) - 2 = x + 8 - 2 = x + 6$

   Substitute x with 4: $(g \circ f)(4) = g(f(x)) = 4 + 6 = 10$

✎ **Using** $f(x) = x + 2$ **and** $g(x) = x - 1$, **find:**

1) $f(g(1))$ 3) $g(f(-1))$

2) $f(f(-2))$ 4) $g(g(2))$

✎ **Using** $f(x) = 5x + 2$ **and** $g(x) = x - 6$, **find:**

5) $f(g(-1))$ 7) $g(f(-2))$

6) $f(f(2))$ 8) $g(g(5))$

Answers – Day 17

Multiplying and Dividing Functions

1) $\frac{1}{6}$
2) -8
3) 6
4) $-\frac{7}{4}$
5) -40
6) $\frac{6}{5}$

Composition of functions

1) 2
2) 2
3) 0
4) 0
5) -33
6) 62
7) -14
8) -7

Day 18: Logarithms

Topics that you'll learn today:

- ✓ Evaluating Logarithms
- ✓ Properties of Logarithms

"The study of mathematics, like the Nile, begins in minuteness but ends in magnificence."

– Charles Caleb Colton

Evaluating Logarithms

Step-by-step guide:

✓ Logarithm is another way of writing exponent. $log_b y = x$ is equivalent to $y = b^x$

✓ Learn some logarithms rules:

$$log_b(x) = \frac{log_d(x)}{log_d(b)}$$

$$log_a a = 1$$

$$log_a x^b = b \, log_a x$$

$$log_a 1 = 0$$

Examples:

1) **Evaluate:** $log_2 16$

   Rewrite 16 in power base form: $16 = 2^4$, then: $log_2 16 = log_2(2^4)$

   Use log rule: $log_a(x^b) = b \cdot log_a(x) \rightarrow log_2(2^4) = 4 log_2(2)$

   Use log rule: $log_a(a) = 1 \rightarrow log_2(2) = 1$. $4 log_2(2) = 4 \times 1 = 4$

2) **Evaluate:** $log_6 216$

   Rewrite 216 in power base form: $216 = 6^3$, then: $log_6 216 = log_6(6^3)$

   Use log rule: $log_a(x^b) = b \cdot log_a(x) \rightarrow log_6(6^3) = 3 log_6(6)$

   Use log rule: $log_a(a) = 1 \rightarrow log_6(6) = 1$. $3 log_6(6) = 3 \times 1 = 3$

✎ *Evaluate each logarithm.*

1) $log_2 8 =$

2) $log_2 \frac{1}{32} =$

3) $log_4 256 =$

4) $log_3 \frac{1}{81} =$

✎ *Circle the points which are on the graph of the given logarithmic functions.*

5) $y = 2 log_3(x + 1) + 2$ (2, 4),   (8, 4),   (0, 3)

6) $y = 3 log_3(3x) - 2$ (3, 6),   (3, 4), $(\frac{1}{3}, 2)$

7) $y = -2 log_2 2(x - 1) + 1$ (3, -3),   (2, 1),   (5, 5)

8) $y = 4 log_4(4x) + 7$ (1, 7),   (1, 11),   (4, 8)

Properties of Logarithms

Step-by-step guide:

✓ Learn some logarithms properties:

$a^{\log_a b} = b$

$\log_a 1 = 0$

$\log_a a = 1$

$\log_a(x \cdot y) = \log_a x + \log_a y$

$\log_a \frac{x}{y} = \log_a x - \log_a y$

$\log_a \frac{1}{x} = -\log_a x$

$\log_a x^p = p \log_a x$

$\log_{x^k} x = \frac{1}{x} \log_a x, \text{ for } k \neq 0$

$\log_a x = \log_{a^c} x^c$

$\log_a x = \frac{1}{\log_x a}$

Examples:

1) **Expand this logarithm.** $\log(2 \times 3) =$

   Use log rule: $\log_a(x \cdot y) = \log_a x + \log_a y$

   Then: $\log(2 \times 3) = \log 2 + \log 3$

2) **Condense this expression to a single logarithm.** $\log 4 - \log 3 =$

   Use log rule: $\log_a x - \log_a y = \log_a \frac{x}{y}$

   Then: $\log 4 - \log 3 = \log \frac{4}{3}$

✏️ *Expand each logarithm.*

1) $\log\left(\frac{1}{2}\right) =$

2) $\log\left(\frac{3}{5}\right) =$

3) $\log\left(\frac{1}{3}\right)^2 =$

4) $\log(8 \times 2^5) =$

5) $\log\left(\frac{2}{7}\right)^3 =$

6) $\log\left(\frac{5^3}{9}\right) =$

✏️ *Condense each expression to a single logarithm.*

7) $\log 2 - \log 5 =$

8) $2 \log 3 - 2 \log 4 =$

9) $4 \log 3 - 4 \log 7 =$

10) $5 \log 2 - 7 \log 9 =$

11) $\log 12 - 6 \log 4 =$

12) $3 \log 14 + 2 \log 18 =$

Answers – Day 18

Evaluating logarithms

1) 3
2) -5
3) 4
4) 4
5) $(2, 4)$
6) $(3, 4)$
7) $(3, -3)$
8) $(1, 11)$

Properties of logarithms

1) $\log 1 - \log 2$
2) $\log 3 - \log 5$
3) $2 \log 1 - 2 \log 3$
4) $\log 8 + 5 \log 2$
5) $3 \log 2 - 3 \log 7$
6) $3 \log 5 - \log 9$
7) $\log \frac{2}{5}$
8) $\log \frac{3^2}{4^2}$
9) $\log \frac{3^4}{7^4}$
10) $\log \frac{2^5}{9^7}$
11) $\log \frac{12}{6^4}$
12) $\log (14^3 18^2)$

Day 19:
Natural Logarithms

Topics that you'll learn today:

- ✓ Natural Logarithms
- ✓ Solving Logarithmic Equations

"A Mathematician who is not also something of a poet will never be a complete mathematician" -Karl Weierstrass

Natural Logarithms

Step-by-step guide:

✓ A natural logarithm is a logarithm that has a special base of the mathematical constant e, which is an irrational number approximately equal to 2.71.
✓ The natural logarithm of x is generally written as $\ln x$, or $\log_e x$.

Examples:

1) **Solve the equation for** x: $e^x = 5$

   If $f(x) = g(x)$, then: $\ln(f(x)) = \ln(g(x)) \to \ln(e^x) = \ln(5)$

   Use log rule: $\log_a x^b = b \log_a x \to \ln(e^x) = x \ln(e) \to x\ln(e) = \ln(5)$

   $\ln(e) = 1$, then: $x = \ln(5)$

2) **Solve equation for** x: $\ln(5x - 1) = 1$

   Use log rule: $a = \log_b(b^a) \to 1 = \ln(e^1) = \ln(e) \to \ln(5x - 1) = \ln(e)$

   When the logs have the same base: $\log_b(f(x)) = \log_b(g(x)) \to f(x) = g(x)$

   $\ln(5x - 1) = \ln(e)$, then: $5x - 1 = e \to x = \frac{e+1}{5}$

✍ **Solve each equation for** x.

1) $e^x = 2$
2) $e^x = 4$
3) $\ln x = 8$
4) $\ln(\ln x) = 3$

5) $e^x = 27$
6) $\ln(3x + 2) = 8$
7) $\ln(9x - 1) = 1$
8) $\ln x = \frac{1}{4}$

✍ **Reduce the following expressions to simplest form.**

9) $e^{\ln 3 + \ln 6} =$

10) $e^{\ln\left(\frac{3}{e}\right)} =$

11) $4 \ln(e^3) =$

12) $\ln\left(\frac{1}{e}\right)^4 =$

Solving Logarithmic Equations

Step-by-step guide:

- ✓ Convert the logarithmic equation to an exponential equation when it's possible. (If no base is indicated, the base of the logarithm is 10)
- ✓ Condense logarithms if you have more than one log on one side of the equation.
- ✓ Plug in the answers back into the original equation and check to see the solution works.

Examples:

1) **Find the value of the variables in each equation.** $\log_2(25 - x^2) = 2$

   Use log rule: $\log_b x = \log_b y$ then: $x = y$

   $2 = \log_2(2^2)$, $\log_4(25 - x^2) = \log_2(2^2) = \log_2 4$

   Then: $25 - x^2 = 4 \to 25 - 16 = x^2 \to x^2 = 9 \to x = 3$

2) **Find the value of the variables in each equation.** $\log(8x + 3) = \log(2x - 6)$

   When the logs have the same base: $f(x) = g(x)$, then: $\ln(f(x)) = \ln(g(x))$

   $\log(8x + 3) = \log(2x - 6) \to 8x + 3 = 2x - 6 \to 8x + 3 - 2x + 6 = 0$

   $6x + 9 = 0 \to 6x = -9 \to x = \dfrac{-9}{6} = -\dfrac{3}{2}$

✎ *Find the value of the variables in each equation.*

1) $\log_5 8x = 0$

2) $\log_4 12x = 2$

3) $\log x + 2 = 1$

4) $\log x - \log 2 = 4$

5) $\log x + \log 8 = 2$

6) $\log 2 + \log x = 0$

7) $\log x + \log 6 = \log 36$

8) $2 \log_2(x - 4) = 4$

9) $\log 3x = \log(x + 6)$

10) $\log(6x - 8) = \log(3x - 1)$

11) $\log(3x - 2) = \log(2x + 1)$

12) $-14 + \log_2(x + 1) = -10$

Answers – Day 19

Natural logarithms

1) $x = \ln 2$
2) $x = \ln 4, x = 2\ln(2)$
3) $x = e^8$
4) $x = e^{e^3}$
5) $x = \ln 27, x = 3\ln(3)$
6) $x = \dfrac{e^8 - 2}{3}$
7) $x = \dfrac{e+1}{9}$
8) $x = \sqrt[4]{e}$
9) 18
10) $\dfrac{3}{e}$
11) 12
12) -4

Solving logarithmic equations

1) $\{\dfrac{1}{8}\}$
2) $\{\dfrac{4}{3}\}$
3) $\{\dfrac{1}{10}\}$
4) $x = 20{,}000$
5) $x = 800$
6) $x = 2$
7) $x = 6$
8) $x = 8$
9) $x = 3$
10) $x = \dfrac{7}{3}$
11) $x = 3$
12) $x = 15$

Day 20: Radical Expressions

Topics that you'll learn today:

- ✓ Simplifying Radical Expressions
- ✓ Simplifying Radical Expressions Involving Fractions

"Without mathematics, there's nothing you can do. Everything around you is mathematics. Everything around you is numbers." – Shakuntala Devi

Simplifying Radical Expressions

Step-by-step guide:

For square roots:

- ✓ Find the prime factors of the numbers inside the radical.
- ✓ Find the largest perfect score factor of the number.
- ✓ Rewrite the radical as the product of perfect score and its matching factor and simplify.

Examples:

1) Find the square root of $\sqrt{169}$.

   First factor the number: $169 = 13^2$, Then: $\sqrt{169} = \sqrt{13^2}$

   Now use radical rule: $\sqrt[n]{a^n} = a$, Then: $\sqrt{13^2} = 13$

2) Evaluate. $\sqrt{9} \times \sqrt{25} =$

   First factor the numbers: $9 = 3^2$ and $25 = 5^2$

   Then: $\sqrt{9} \times \sqrt{25} = \sqrt{3^2} \times \sqrt{5^2}$

   Now use radical rule: $\sqrt[n]{a^n} = a$, Then: $\sqrt{3^2} \times \sqrt{5^2} = 3 \times 5 = 15$

🖎 Simplify.

1) $\sqrt{25x^2}$

2) $\sqrt{900x^2}$

3) $\sqrt{100x^2}$

4) $\sqrt{125a}$

5) $\sqrt{216v}$

6) $\sqrt{450x^2}$

7) $\sqrt{405}$

8) $\sqrt{512p^3}$

9) $\sqrt{216m^4}$

10) $\sqrt{264x^3y^3}$

11) $\sqrt{49x^3y^3}$

12) $\sqrt{16a^4b^3}$

Simplifying Radical Expressions Involving Fractions

Step-by-step guide:

- ✓ Radical expressions cannot be in the denominator. (number in the bottom)
- ✓ To get rid of the radical in the denominator, multiply both numerator and denominator by the radical in the denominator.
- ✓ If there is a radical and another integer in the denominator, multiply both numerator and denominator by the conjugate of the denominator.
- ✓ The conjugate of a + b is a-b and vice versa.

Examples:

1) Simplify $\dfrac{2}{\sqrt{3} - 2}$

   Multiply by the conjugate: $\dfrac{\sqrt{3} + 2}{\sqrt{3} + 2} \rightarrow \dfrac{2}{\sqrt{3} - 2} \times \dfrac{\sqrt{3} + 2}{\sqrt{3} + 2}$

   $(\sqrt{3} - 2)(\sqrt{3} + 2) = -1$ then: $\dfrac{2(\sqrt{3} + 2)}{-1}$

   Use the fraction rule: $\dfrac{a}{-b} = -\dfrac{a}{b} \rightarrow \dfrac{2(\sqrt{3} + 2)}{-1} = -\dfrac{2(\sqrt{3} + 2)}{1} = -2(\sqrt{3} + 2)$

2) Simplify $\dfrac{3}{\sqrt{7} - 2}$

   Multiply by the conjugate: $\dfrac{\sqrt{7}+2}{\sqrt{7}+2}$

   $\dfrac{3}{\sqrt{7} - 2} \times \dfrac{\sqrt{7}+2}{\sqrt{7}+2} = \dfrac{3(\sqrt{7}+2)}{3} \rightarrow \dfrac{3(\sqrt{7}+2)}{3} = \sqrt{7} + 2$

✍ Simplify.

1) $\dfrac{\sqrt{5m}}{\sqrt{m^3}}$

2) $\dfrac{8\sqrt{6}}{\sqrt{x}}$

3) $\dfrac{\sqrt{5} - \sqrt{3}}{\sqrt{3} - \sqrt{5}}$

4) $\dfrac{5\sqrt{3} - 3\sqrt{2}}{3\sqrt{2} - 2\sqrt{3}}$

5) $\dfrac{\sqrt{31x^5y^3}}{\sqrt{2xy^2}}$

6) $\dfrac{6\sqrt{45k^3}}{3\sqrt{5k}}$

7) $\dfrac{\sqrt{a}}{\sqrt{a} + \sqrt{b}}$

8) $\dfrac{2}{3 + \sqrt{7}}$

9) $\dfrac{1 + \sqrt{2}}{3 + \sqrt{5}}$

10) $\dfrac{2 + \sqrt{5}}{6 - \sqrt{3}}$

11) $\dfrac{\sqrt{7} + \sqrt{5}}{\sqrt{5} + \sqrt{2}}$

12) $\dfrac{3\sqrt{2} - \sqrt{7}}{4\sqrt{2} + \sqrt{5}}$

Answers – Day 20

Simplifying radical expressions

1) $5x$
2) $30x$
3) $10x$
4) $5\sqrt{5a}$
5) $6\sqrt{6v}$
6) $15x\sqrt{2}$
7) $9\sqrt{5}$
8) $16p\sqrt{2p}$
9) $6m^2\sqrt{6}$
10) $2x.y\sqrt{66xy}$
11) $7x.y\sqrt{xy}$
12) $2a^2.b\sqrt{2b}$

Simplifying Radical Expressions Involving Fractions

1) $\frac{\sqrt{5}}{m}$
2) $\frac{8\sqrt{6x}}{x}$
3) -1
4) $\frac{3\sqrt{6}+4}{2}$
5) $4x^2\sqrt{y}$
6) $6k$
7) $\frac{a-\sqrt{ab}}{a-b}$
8) $3-\sqrt{7}$
9) $\frac{3-\sqrt{5}+3\sqrt{2}-\sqrt{10}}{4}$
10) $\frac{12+2\sqrt{3}+6\sqrt{5}+\sqrt{15}}{33}$
11) $\frac{\sqrt{35}-\sqrt{14}+5\sqrt{10}}{3}$
12) $\frac{24-3\sqrt{10}-4\sqrt{14}+\sqrt{35}}{27}$

Day 21: Radical Expressions Operations

Topics that you'll learn today:

- ✓ Multiplying Radical Expressions
- ✓ Adding and Subtracting Radical Expressions

Mathematics is like checkers in being suitable for the young, not too difficult, amusing, and without peril to the state. – Plato

Multiplying Radical Expressions

Step-by-step guide:

- ✓ To multiply radical expressions:
- ✓ Multiply the numbers outside of the radicals.
- ✓ Multiply the numbers inside the radicals.
- ✓ Simplify if needed.

Examples:

1) **Evaluate.** $\sqrt{16} \times \sqrt{9} =$

   First factor the numbers: $16 = 4^2$ and $9 = 3^2$

   Then: $\sqrt{16} \times \sqrt{9} = \sqrt{4^2} \times \sqrt{3^2}$

   Now use radical rule: $\sqrt[n]{a^n} = a$, Then: $\sqrt{4^2} \times \sqrt{3^2} = 4 \times 3 = 12$

2) **Evaluate.** $2\sqrt{5} \times 3\sqrt{2} =$

   Multiply the numbers: $2 \times 3 = 6$

   $2\sqrt{5} \times 3\sqrt{2} = 6\sqrt{5}\sqrt{2}$

   Use radical rule: $\sqrt{a}\sqrt{b} = \sqrt{ab} \to 6\sqrt{5}\sqrt{2} = 6\sqrt{5 \times 2} = 6\sqrt{10}$

☞ *Simplify.*

1) $\sqrt{4} \times 2\sqrt{9} =$

2) $2\sqrt{25} \times 3\sqrt{81} =$

3) $5\sqrt{49} \times 4\sqrt{16} =$

4) $2\sqrt{64} \times 7\sqrt{36} =$

5) $8\sqrt{16} \times 3\sqrt{100} =$

6) $-5\sqrt{12} \times -\sqrt{3} =$

7) $\sqrt{23a^2} \times \sqrt{23a} =$

8) $2\sqrt{20k^2} \times \sqrt{5k^2} =$

9) $\sqrt{12x^2} \times \sqrt{2x^3} =$

10) $12\sqrt{7x} \times \sqrt{5x^3} =$

11) $4\sqrt{9x^3} \times 7\sqrt{3x^2} =$

12) $3\sqrt{40x^5} \times 9\sqrt{2x} =$

Adding and Subtracting Radical Expressions

Step-by-step guide:

- ✓ Only numbers that have the same radical part can be added or subtracted.
- ✓ Remember, combining "unlike" radical terms is not possible.
- ✓ For number with the same radical part, just add or subtract factors outside the radicals.

Examples:

1) Simplify $4\sqrt{5} + 3\sqrt{5} =$

   Add like terms: $4\sqrt{5} + 3\sqrt{5} = 7\sqrt{5}$

2) Simplify $2\sqrt{7} + 4\sqrt{7} =$

   Add like terms: $2\sqrt{7} + 4\sqrt{7} = 6\sqrt{7}$

✎ **Simplify.**

1) $9\sqrt{5} + 4\sqrt{5} =$

2) $4\sqrt{20} - 3\sqrt{20} =$

3) $3\sqrt{22} - 4\sqrt{22} =$

4) $14\sqrt{7} + 12\sqrt{7} =$

5) $4\sqrt{3} - \sqrt{27} =$

6) $\sqrt{12} + 5\sqrt{3} =$

7) $-3\sqrt{15} + 3\sqrt{15} =$

8) $-12\sqrt{8} + 3\sqrt{2} =$

9) $5\sqrt{45} - 3\sqrt{5} =$

10) $-3\sqrt{18} - 2\sqrt{2} =$

11) $16\sqrt{35} + 10\sqrt{35} =$

12) $13\sqrt{19} - 7\sqrt{19} =$

Answers – Day 21

Multiplying radical expressions

1) 12
2) 270
3) 560
4) 672
5) 960
6) 30
7) $23a\sqrt{a}$
8) $4k^2\sqrt{10k}$
9) $2x^2\sqrt{6x}$
10) $12x^2\sqrt{35}$
11) $84x^2\sqrt{3x}$
12) $108x^3\sqrt{5}$

Adding and Subtracting Radical Expressions

1) $13\sqrt{5}$
2) $\sqrt{20}$
3) $-\sqrt{22}$
4) $26\sqrt{7}$
5) $\sqrt{3}$
6) $7\sqrt{3}$
7) 0
8) $-21\sqrt{2}$
9) $12\sqrt{5}$
10) $-11\sqrt{2}$
11) $26\sqrt{35}$
12) $6\sqrt{19}$

Day 22:
Radical Functions

Topics that you'll learn today:

- ✓ Domain and Range of Radical Functions
- ✓ Radical Equations

"It's fine to work on any problem, so long as it generates interesting mathematics along the way – even if you don't solve it at the end of the day." – Andrew Wiles

Domain and Range of Radical Functions

Step-by-step guide:

- ✓ To find domain and rage of radical functions, remember that having a negative number under the square root symbol is not possible. (for square roots)
- ✓ To find the domain of the function, find all possible values of the variable inside radical.
- ✓ To find the range, plugin the minimum and maximum values of the variable inside radical.

Examples:

Find the domain and range of the radical function. $y = \sqrt{x-2}$

For domain: Find non-negative values for radicals: $x \geq 2$

$\sqrt{f(x)} \to f(x) \geq 0$

Then solve $x - 2 \geq 0 \to x \geq 2$

domain: $x \geq 2$

for range: the range of an radical function of the form $c\sqrt{ax+b} + k$ is $f(x) \geq k$

$k = 0$ then: $f(x) \geq 0$

✐ Identify the domain and range of each.

1) $y = \sqrt{x+5}$

2) $y = \sqrt{x-1} - 1$

3) $y = \sqrt{x-3} + 7$

4) $y = \sqrt{x+1} - 4$

✐ Sketch the graph of each function.

5) $y = \sqrt{x} + 2$

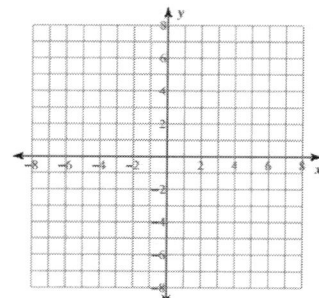

6) $y = 2\sqrt{x} - 5$

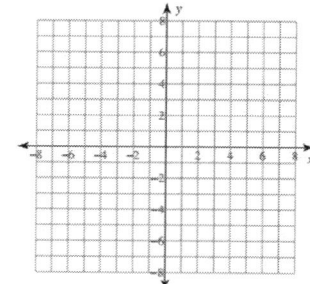

Radical Equations

Step-by-step guide:

- ✓ Isolate the radical on one side of the equation.
- ✓ Square both sides of the equation to remove the radical
- ✓ Solve the equation for the variable
- ✓ Plugin the answer into the original equation to avoid extraneous values.

Examples:

1) Solve $\sqrt{x} - 8 = 12$

   Add 8 to both sides: $\sqrt{x} = 20$

   Square both sides: $(\sqrt{x})^2 = 20^2 \rightarrow x = 400$

2) Solve $\sqrt{x+2} = 6$

   Square both sides: $(\sqrt{(x+2)})^2 = 6^2 \rightarrow x + 2 = 36 \rightarrow x = 34$

✎ *Solve each equation. Remember to check for extraneous solutions.*

1) $\sqrt{x-4} = 2$

2) $6 = \sqrt{x-5}$

3) $\sqrt{x+8} = 12$

4) $\sqrt{x+14} = 10$

5) $9 = \sqrt{x-8}$

6) $21 = \sqrt{x-5}$

7) $12 = \sqrt{x+4}$

8) $2\sqrt{x+8} = 14$

9) $\sqrt{x+5} - 1 = 16$

10) $\sqrt{2x} = \sqrt{3x-8}$

11) $\sqrt{4x+10} = \sqrt{x+12}$

12) $\sqrt{x} = \sqrt{2x-16}$

Answers – Day 22

Domain and Range of Radical Functions

1) domain: $x \geq -5$
   range: $y \geq 0$

2) domain: {all real numbers}
   range: {all real numbers}

3) domain: $x \geq 3$
   range: $y \geq 7$

4) domain: {all real numbers}
   range: {all real numbers}

5)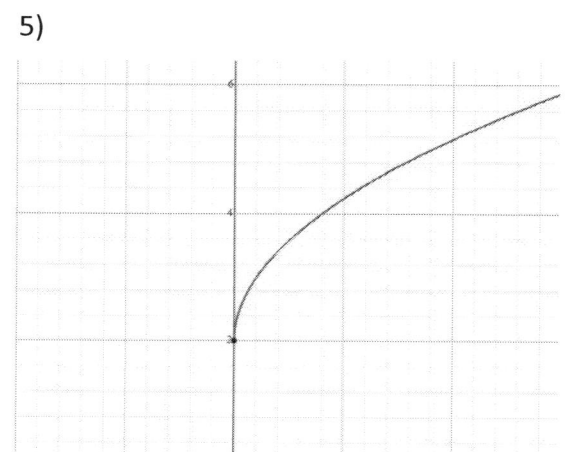

6)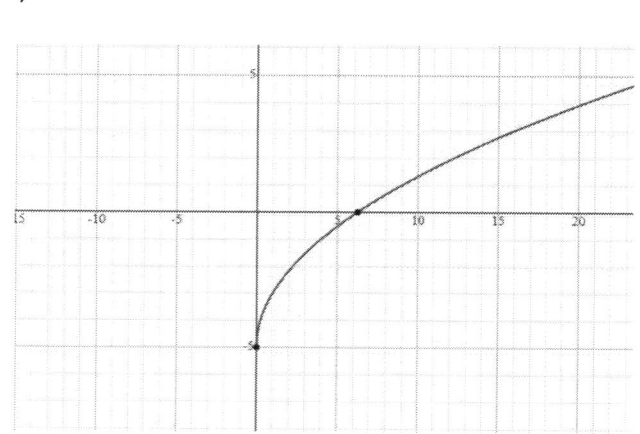

Radical Equations

1) {8}
2) {41}
3) {136}
4) {86}
5) {89}
6) {446}
7) {140}
8) {41}
9) {284}
10) {8}
11) $\{\frac{2}{3}\}$
12) {16}

Day 23:
Rational Expressions

Topics that you'll learn today:

- ✓ Simplifying Rational Expressions
- ✓ Graphing Rational Expressions

Mathematics is the door and key to the sciences. – Roger Bacon

Simplifying Rational Expressions

Step-by-step guide:

- ✓ Factorize numerator and denominator if they are factorable.
- ✓ Find common factors of both numerator and denominator.
- ✓ Remove the common factor in both numerator and denominator.
- ✓ Simplify if needed.

Examples:

1) Simplify $\frac{9x^2y}{3y^2}$

   Cancel the common factor 3: $\frac{9x^2y}{3y^2} = \frac{3x^2y}{y^2}$

   Cancel the common factor y: $\frac{3x^2y}{y^2} = \frac{3x^2}{y}$

   Then: $\frac{9x^2y}{3y^2} = \frac{3x^2}{y}$

2) Simplify $\frac{x^2+5x-6}{x+6}$

   Factor $x^2 + 5x - 6 = (x - 1)(x + 6)$

   Then: $\frac{x^2+5x-6}{x+6} = \frac{(x-1)(x+6)}{x+6}$

   Cancel the common factor: $(x + 6)$

   Then: $\frac{(x-1)(x+6)}{x+6} = x - 1$

✍ Simplify.

1) $\frac{16x^3}{20x^3} =$

2) $\frac{64x^3}{24x} =$

3) $\frac{25x^5}{15x^3} =$

4) $\frac{16}{2x - 2} =$

5) $\frac{15x-3}{24} =$

6) $\frac{4x + 16}{28} =$

7) $\frac{x^2 - 10x+25}{x - 5} =$

8) $\frac{x^2-49}{x^2+3x-28} =$

9) $\frac{x^2+4x+4}{x^2-5x-14} =$

Graphing Rational Expressions

Step-by-step guide:
- ✓ Find the vertical asymptotes of the function, if there is any. (Vertical asymptotes are vertical lines which correspond to the zeroes of the denominator)
- ✓ Find horizontal or slant asymptote. (If numerator has a bigger degree than denominator, there will be slant asymptote.)
- ✓ If denominator has a bigger degree than numerator, the horizontal asymptote is the x-axes or the line y=0. If they have the same degree, the horizontal asymptote equals the leading coefficient (the coefficient of the largest exponent) of the numerator divided by the leading coefficient of the denominator.
- ✓ Find intercepts and plug in some values of x and solve for y and graph

Examples:

Graph rational expressions. $f(x) = \frac{x^2-x+2}{x-1}$

Domain: $\begin{bmatrix} solution: x < 1 \ or \ x > 1 \\ interval \ notation: (-\infty, 1) \cup (1, \infty) \end{bmatrix}$

Range:
$\begin{bmatrix} solution: f(x) \leq -2\sqrt{6} + 3 \ or \ f(x) \geq 2\sqrt{6} + 3 \\ interval \ notation: (-\infty, -2\sqrt{6} + 3] \cup [2\sqrt{6} + 3, \infty) \end{bmatrix}$

Axis interception points of $\frac{x^2-x+2}{x-1}$: y Interceptions: $(0, -2)$

Asymptotes of $\frac{x^2-x+2}{x-1}$: vertical: $x = 1$, horizontal: $y = 2x + 1$

Extreme points of $\frac{x^2-x+2}{x-1}$: Maximum $(\frac{2-\sqrt{6}}{2}, -\frac{4\sqrt{3}-3\sqrt{2}}{\sqrt{2}})$, Minimum $(\frac{2+\sqrt{6}}{2}, \frac{4\sqrt{3}+3\sqrt{2}}{\sqrt{2}})$

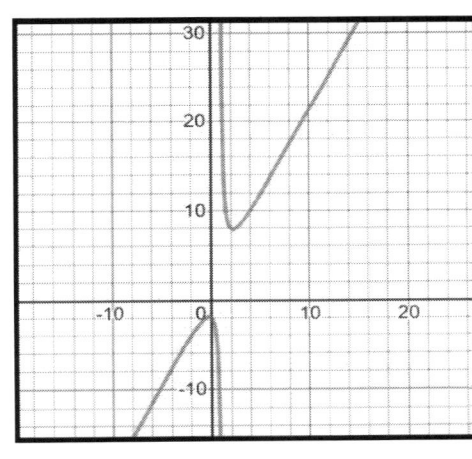

✍ Graph rational expressions.

1) $f(x) = \frac{x^2 + 2x - 4}{x - 2}$

2) $f(x) = \frac{4x^3 - 16x + 64}{x^2 - 2x - 4}$

Answers – Day 23

Simplifying rational expressions

1) $\dfrac{4}{5}$

2) $\dfrac{8x^2}{3}$

3) $\dfrac{5x^2}{3}$

4) $\dfrac{8}{x-1}$

5) $\dfrac{5x-1}{8}$

6) $\dfrac{x+4}{7}$

7) $x-5$

8) $\dfrac{x-7}{x-4}$

9) $\dfrac{x+2}{x-7}$

Graphing rational expressions

1)

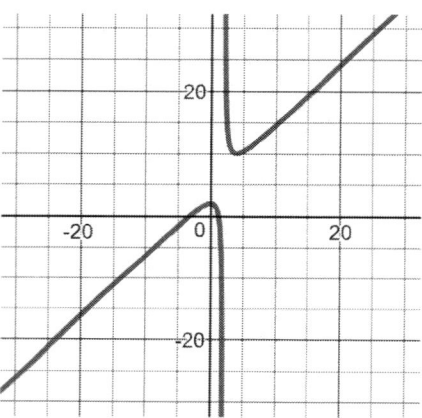

2)

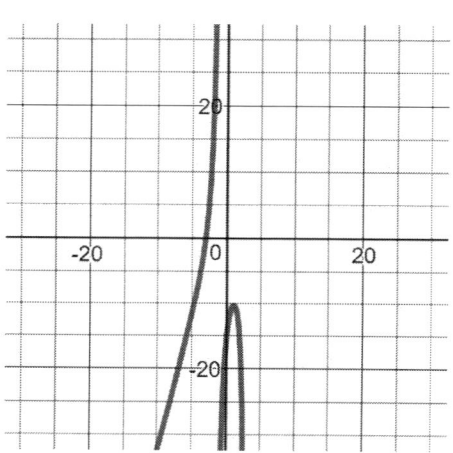

Day 24: Multiplying and Dividing Rational Expressions

Topics that you'll learn today:

- ✓ Multiplying Rational Expressions
- ✓ Dividing Rational Expressions

Mathematics is an independent world created out of pure intelligence.

~ William Woods Worth

Multiplying Rational Expressions

Step-by-step guide:

✓ Multiplying rational expressions is the same as multiplying fractions. First, multiply numerators and then multiply denominators. Then, simplify as needed.

Examples:

1) Solve $\frac{x+4}{x-2} \times \frac{x-2}{3} =$

   Multiply fractions: $\frac{x+4}{x-2} \times \frac{x-2}{3} = \frac{(x+4)(x-2)}{3(x-2)}$

   Cancel the common factor: $(x-2)$

   then: $\frac{(x+4)(x-2)}{3(x-2)} = \frac{(x+4)}{3}$

2) Solve $\frac{x-5}{x+3} \times \frac{2x+6}{x-5} =$

   Multiply fractions: $\frac{x-5}{x+3} \times \frac{2x+6}{x-5} = \frac{(x-5)(2x+6)}{(x+3)(x-5)}$

   Cancel the common factor: $\frac{(x-5)(2x+6)}{(x+3)(x-5)} = \frac{(2x+6)}{(x+3)}$

   Factor $2x + 6 = 2(x+3)$

   Then: $\frac{2(x+3)}{(x+3)} = 2$

✎ Simplify each expression.

1) $\frac{79x}{25} \cdot \frac{85}{27x^2} =$

2) $\frac{96}{38x} \cdot \frac{25}{45} =$

3) $\frac{84}{3} \cdot \frac{48x}{95} =$

4) $\frac{53}{43} \cdot \frac{46x^2}{31} =$

5) $\frac{93}{21x} \cdot \frac{34x}{51x} =$

6) $\frac{5x+50}{x+10} \cdot \frac{x-2}{5} =$

7) $\frac{x-7}{x+6} \cdot \frac{10x+60}{x-7} =$

8) $\frac{1}{x+10} \cdot \frac{10x+30}{x+3} =$

Dividing Rational Expressions

Step-by-step guide:

- ✓ To divide rational expression, use the same method we use for dividing fractions.
- ✓ Keep, Change, Flip
- ✓ Keep first rational expression, change division sign to multiplication, and flip the numerator and denominator of the second rational expression. Then, multiply numerators and multiply denominators. Simplify as needed.

Examples:

1) Solve $\dfrac{8x}{5} \div \dfrac{12}{7} =$

$\dfrac{8x}{5} \div \dfrac{12}{7} = \dfrac{\frac{8x}{5}}{\frac{12}{7}}$, Use Divide fractions rules: $\dfrac{\frac{a}{b}}{\frac{c}{d}} = \dfrac{a \cdot d}{b \cdot c}$

$\dfrac{\frac{8x}{5}}{\frac{12}{7}} = \dfrac{8x \times 7}{12 \times 5} = \dfrac{56x}{60}$

2) Solve $\dfrac{2x}{x+5} \div \dfrac{x}{2x+10} =$

$\dfrac{\frac{2x}{x+5}}{\frac{x}{2x+10}}$, Use Divide fractions rules: $\dfrac{(2x)(2x+10)}{(x)(x+5)}$

Cancel common fraction: $\dfrac{(2x)(2x+10)}{(x)(x+5)} = \dfrac{2(2x+10)}{(x+5)} = \dfrac{4(x+5)}{(x+5)} = 4$

✏️ Divide.

1) $\dfrac{12x}{3} \div \dfrac{5}{8} =$

2) $\dfrac{10x^2}{7} \div \dfrac{3x}{12} =$

3) $\dfrac{x+5}{5x^2 - 10x} \div \dfrac{1}{5x} =$

4) $\dfrac{x-2}{x+6x-12} \div \dfrac{x}{x+3} =$

5) $\dfrac{5x}{x-10} \div \dfrac{5x}{x-5} =$

6) $\dfrac{x^2 + 10x + 16}{x^2 + 6x + 8} \div \dfrac{1}{x+8} =$

7) $\dfrac{x^2 - 2x - 15}{8x + 20} \div \dfrac{2}{4x + 10} =$

8) $\dfrac{x-4}{x^2 - 2x - 8} \div \dfrac{1}{x-5} =$

Answers – Day 24

Multiplying rational expressions

1) $\dfrac{1343}{135x}$
2) $\dfrac{80}{57x}$
3) $\dfrac{1344x}{95}$
4) $\dfrac{2438x^2}{1333}$
5) $\dfrac{62}{21x}$
6) $x-2$
7) 10
8) $\dfrac{10}{x+10}$

Dividing rational expressions

1) $6x^2$
2) $\dfrac{40x}{7}$
3) $\dfrac{x+5}{x-2}$
4) $\dfrac{(x-2)(x+3)}{x(7x-12)}$
5) $\dfrac{x^2}{(x-10)(x-5)}$
6) $x+8$
7) $\dfrac{(x+3)(x-5)}{4}$
8) $\dfrac{x-5}{x+2}$

Day 25: Adding and Subtracting Rational Expressions

Topics that you'll learn today:

- ✓ Adding and Subtracting Rational Expressions
- ✓ Rational Equations

"Millions saw the apple fall, but Newton asked why." – Bernard Baruch

Adding and Subtracting Rational Expressions

Step-by-step guide:

- ✓ For adding and subtracting rational expressions:
- ✓ Find least common denominator (LCD).
- ✓ Write each expression using the LCD.
- ✓ Add or subtract the numerators.
- ✓ Simplify as needed.

Examples:

1) Solve $\dfrac{3}{2x+5} + \dfrac{x-2}{2x+5} =$

   Use this rule: $\dfrac{a}{c} \pm \dfrac{b}{c} = \dfrac{a \pm b}{c} \rightarrow \dfrac{3}{2x+5} + \dfrac{x-2}{2x+5} = \dfrac{3(x-2)}{2x+5} = \dfrac{3x-6}{2x+5}$

2) Solve $\dfrac{x+4}{x-8} + \dfrac{x-4}{x+6} =$

   Least common multiplier of $(x-8)$ and $(x+6)$: $(x-8)(x+6)$

   Then: $\dfrac{(x+4)(x+6)}{(x-8)(x+6)} + \dfrac{(x-4)(x-8)}{(x+6)(x-8)} = \dfrac{(x+4)(x+6)+(x-4)(x-8)}{(x+6)(x-6)}$

   Expand: $(x+4)(x+6) + (x-4)(x-8) = 2x^2 - 2x + 56$

   Then: $\dfrac{2x^2 - 2x + 56}{(x+6)(x-8)}$

✎ Simplify each expression.

1) $\dfrac{2}{6x+10} + \dfrac{x-6}{6x+10} =$

2) $\dfrac{4}{x+1} - \dfrac{2}{x+2} =$

3) $\dfrac{2x}{5x+4} + \dfrac{6x}{2x+3} =$

4) $\dfrac{4x}{x+2} + \dfrac{x-3}{x+1} =$

5) $\dfrac{x}{3x+2} + \dfrac{3x}{2x+3} =$

6) $\dfrac{x+5}{4x^2+20x} - \dfrac{x-5}{4x^2+20x} =$

7) $\dfrac{2}{x^2-5x+4} + \dfrac{2}{x^2-4} =$

8) $\dfrac{x-7}{x^2-16} - \dfrac{x-1}{16-x^2} =$

Rational Equations

Step-by-step guide:

- ✓ For solving rational equations, we can use following methods:
- ✓ Converting to a common denominator: In this method, you need to get a common denominator for both sides of equation Then make numerators equal and solve for the variable.
- ✓ Cross-multiplying: This method is useful when there is only one fraction on each side of the equation. Simply multiply first numerator by second denominator and make the result equal to the product of second numerator and first denominator.

Examples: Solve $\frac{x-2}{x+1} = \frac{x+5}{x-2}$

Use fraction cross multiply: if $\frac{a}{b} = \frac{c}{d}$ then: $a.d = b.c$
Then: $(x-2)(x-2) = (x+5)(x+1)$
Simplify: $(x-2)^2 = (x+5)(x+1)$
Expand: $(x-2)^2 = x^2 - 4x + 4$
Expand: $(x+5)(x+1) = x^2 + 6x + 5$
Then: $x^2 - 4x + 4 = x^2 + 6x + 5$
Simplify: $x^2 - 4x = x^2 + 6x + 1$
Subtract both sides: $x^2 + 6x$
Then: $-10x = 1 \rightarrow x = -\frac{1}{10}$

✍ *Solve each equation. Remember to check for extraneous solutions.*

1) $\frac{2x-3}{x+1} = \frac{x+6}{x-2}$

2) $\frac{3x-2}{9x+1} = \frac{2x-5}{6x-5}$

3) $\frac{1}{n-8} - 1 = \frac{7}{n-8}$

4) $\frac{x+5}{x^2-2x} - 1 = \frac{1}{x^2-2x}$

5) $\frac{x-2}{x+3} - 1 = \frac{1}{x+2}$

6) $\frac{1}{6x^2} = \frac{1}{3x^2} - \frac{1}{x}$

7) $\frac{x+5}{x^2-x} = \frac{1}{x^2+x} - \frac{x-6}{x+1}$

8) $1 = \frac{1}{x^2-2x} + \frac{x-1}{x}$

Answers – Day 25

Adding and subtracting rational expressions

1) $\frac{-4+x}{6x+10}$

2) $\frac{2x+6}{(x+1)(x+2)}$

3) $\frac{34x^2+30x}{(5x+4)(2x+3)}$

4) $\frac{5x^2+3x-6}{(x+2)(x+1)}$

5) $\frac{11x^2+9x}{(3x+2)(2x+3)}$

6) $\frac{5}{2x(x+5)}$

7) $\frac{4x^2-10x}{(x-1)(x-4)(x+2)(x-2)}$

8) $\frac{2}{x+4}$

Rational Equations

1) $\{0, 14\}$

2) $\{\frac{1}{6}\}$

3) $\{2\}$

4) $\{4, -1\}$

5) $\{-\frac{19}{8}\}$

6) $\{\frac{1}{6}\}$

7) $\{-\frac{1}{4}\}$

8) $\{4, 1\}$

Day 26:
Complex Fractions

Topics that you'll learn today:

✓ Simplify Complex Fractions

Mathematics is like checkers in being suitable for the young, not too difficult, amusing, and without peril to the state. – Plato

Simplify Complex Fractions

- ✓ Convert mixed numbers to improper fractions.
- ✓ Simplify all fractions.
- ✓ Write the fraction in the numerator of the main fraction line then write division sing (÷) and the fraction of the denominator.
- ✓ Use normal method for dividing fractions.
- ✓ Simplify as needed.

Examples: Solve $\dfrac{\frac{2}{5}}{\frac{2}{25} - \frac{5}{16}}$

Use the fraction rule: $\dfrac{\frac{b}{c}}{a} = \dfrac{b}{c \cdot a}$

$$\dfrac{\frac{2}{5}}{\frac{2}{25} - \frac{5}{16}} = \dfrac{2}{5(\frac{2}{25} - \frac{5}{16})} = \dfrac{2}{5(-\frac{93}{400})} = \dfrac{2}{-5 \cdot \frac{93}{400}} = -\dfrac{2}{5 \cdot \frac{93}{400}} = -\dfrac{2}{\frac{93}{80}}$$

Use the fraction rule: $\dfrac{a}{\frac{b}{c}} = \dfrac{a \cdot c}{b} \rightarrow -\dfrac{2}{\frac{93}{80}} = -\dfrac{2 \cdot 80}{93} = -\dfrac{160}{93}$

✍ *Simplify each expression.*

1) $\dfrac{\frac{12}{3}}{\frac{2}{15}} =$

2) $\dfrac{8}{\frac{8}{x} + \frac{2}{3x}} =$

3) $\dfrac{x}{\frac{2}{5} - \frac{2}{x}} =$

4) $\dfrac{\frac{2}{x+2}}{\frac{8}{x^2+6x+8}} =$

5) $\dfrac{\frac{12}{x-1}}{\frac{12}{5} - \frac{12}{25}} =$

6) $\dfrac{1 + \frac{2}{x-4}}{1 - \frac{6}{x-4}} =$

7) $\dfrac{\frac{x+6}{4}}{\frac{x^2}{2} - \frac{5}{2}} =$

8) $\dfrac{\frac{x-2}{x-6}}{\frac{8}{x-2} + \frac{2}{9}} =$

Answers – Day 26

Simplify complex fractions

1) 30

2) $\dfrac{12x}{13}$

3) $\dfrac{5x^2}{2x-10}$

4) $\dfrac{(x+4)}{4}$

5) $\dfrac{25}{4x-4}$

6) $\dfrac{x-2}{x-10}$

7) $\dfrac{x+6}{2x^2-10}$

8) $\dfrac{9(x-2)^2}{(2x+68(x-6)}$

Day 27: Arithmetic and Geometric Sequences

Math Topics that you'll learn today:

- ✓ Arithmetic Sequences
- ✓ Geometric Sequences

Mathematics is like checkers in being suitable for the young, not too difficult, amusing, and without peril to the state. –

Plato

Arithmetic Sequences

Step-by-step guide:

✓ A sequence of numbers such that the difference between the consecutive terms is constant is called arithmetic sequence. For example, the sequence 6, 8, 10, 12, 14, ... is an arithmetic sequence with common difference of 2.
✓ To find any term in an arithmetic sequence use this formula: $x_n = a + d(n-1)$
a = the first term, d = the common difference between terms, n = number of items

Examples:

1) Find the first three terms of the sequence. $a_{17} = 38, d = 3$

First, we need to find a_1 or a. Use arithmetic sequence formula: $x_n = a + d(n-1)$

If $a_8 = 38$, then $n = 8$. Rewrite the formula and put the values provided:

$x_n = a + d(n-1) \to 38 = a + 3(3-1) = a + 6$, now solve for a.

$38 = a + 6 \to a = 38 - 6 = 32$,

First Five Terms: 32, 35, 38

2) Given the first term and the common difference of an arithmetic sequence find the first five terms. $a_1 = 18, d = 2$

Use arithmetic sequence formula: $x_n = a + d(n-1)$,

If $n = 1$ then: $x_1 = 18 + 2(1) \to x_1 = 18$

First Five Terms: 18, 20, 22, 24, 26

✍ *Find the next three terms of each arithmetic sequence.*

1) $15, 11, 7, 3, -1, ...$

2) $-21, -14, -7, 0, ...$

3) $3, 6, 9, 12, 15, ...$

4) $4, 8, 12, 16, 20, ...$

✍ *Given the first term and the common difference of an arithmetic sequence find the first five terms and the explicit formula.*

5) $a_1 = 24, d = 2$

6) $a_1 = -15, d = -5$

7) $a_1 = 18, d = 10$

8) $a_1 = -38, d = -10$

Geometric Sequences

Step-by-step guide:

✓ It is a sequence of numbers where each term after the first is found by multiplying the previous item by the common ratio, a fixed, non-zero number. For example, the sequence 2, 4, 8, 16, 32, ... is a geometric sequence with common ratio of 2.

✓ To find any term in a geometric sequence use this formula: $x_n = ar^{(n-1)}$

a = the first term, r = the common ratio, n = number of items

Examples:

1) Given the first term and the common ratio of a geometric sequence find the first five terms of the sequence. $a_1 = 3, r = -2$

Use geometric sequence formula: $x_n = ar^{(n-1)} \to x_n = 0.8 \cdot (-5)^{n-1}$

If $n = 1$ then: $x_1 = 3 \cdot (-2)^{1-1} = 3(1) = 3$, First Five Terms: $3, -6, 12, -24, 48$

2) Given two terms in a geometric sequence find the 8th term. $a_3 = 10$ **and** $a_5 = 40$

Use geometric sequence formula: $x_n = ar^{(n-1)} \to a_3 = ar^{(3-1)} = ar^2 = 10$

$$x_n = ar^{(n-1)} \to a_5 = ar^{(5-1)} = ar^4 = 40$$

Now divide a_5 by a_3. Then: $\frac{a_5}{a_3} = \frac{ar^4}{ar^2} = \frac{40}{10}$, Now simplify: $\frac{ar^4}{ar^2} = \frac{40}{10} \to r^2 = 4 \to r = 2$

We can find a now: $ar^2 = 12 \to a(2^2) = 10 \to a = 2.5$

Use the formula to find the 8th term: $x_n = ar^{(n-1)} \to a_8 = (2.5)(2)^8 = 2.5(256) = 640$

✎ *Determine if the sequence is geometric. If it is, find the common ratio.*

1) $1, -5, 25, -125, ...$
2) $-2, -4, -8, -16, ...$

3) $4, 16, 36, 64, ...$
4) $-3, -15, -75, -375, ...$

✎ *Given the first term and the common ratio of a geometric sequence find the first five terms and the explicit formula.*

5) $a_1 = 0.8, r = -5$
6) $a_1 = 1, r = 2$

Answers – Day 27

Arithmetic Sequences

1) $-5, -9, -13$
2) $7, 14, 21$
3) $18, 21, 24$
4) $24, 28, 32$
5) First Five Terms: $24, 26, 28, 30, 32$, Explicit: $a_n = 2n + 22$
6) First Five Terms: $-15, -20, -25, -30, -35$, Explicit: $a_n = -5n - 10$
7) First Five Terms: $18, 28, 38, 48, 58$, Explicit: $a_n = 10n + 8$
8) First Five Terms: $-38, -138, -238, -338, -438$, Explicit: $a_n = -100n + 62$

Geometric Sequences

1) $r = -5$
2) $r = 2$
3) not geometric
4) $r = 5$
5) First Five Terms: $0.8, -4, 20, -100, 500$

   Explicit: $a_n = 0.8 \cdot (-5)^{n-1}$

6) First Five Terms: $1, 2, 4, 8, 16$

   Explicit: $a_n = 2^{n-1}$

Day 28:
Finite and Infinite Geometric Series

Math Topics that you'll learn today:

✓ Finite Geometric Series

✓ Infinite Geometric Series

Mathematics is like checkers in being suitable for the young, not too difficult, amusing, and without peril to the state. –

Plato

Finite Geometric Series

Step-by-step guide:

✓ The sum of a geometric series is finite when the absolute value of the ratio is less than 1.
✓ Finite Geometric Series formula: $S_n = \sum_{i=1}^{n} ar^{i-1} = a_1\left(\frac{1-r^n}{1-r}\right)$

Examples:

Evaluate each geometric series described.

1) $\sum_{n=1}^{5} 3^{n-1}$

Use this formula: $S_n = \sum_{i=1}^{n} ar^{i-1} = a_1\left(\frac{1-r^n}{1-r}\right) \to \sum_{n=1}^{5} 3^{n-1} = (1)\left(\frac{1-3^5}{1-3}\right)$

$\to (1)\left(\frac{1-3^5}{1-3}\right) = 121$

2) $\sum_{n=1}^{3} -4^{n-1}$

Use this formula: $S_n = \sum_{i=1}^{n} ar^{i-1} = a_1\left(\frac{1-r^n}{1-r}\right) \to \sum_{n=1}^{3} -4^{n-1} = (-1)\left(\frac{1-4^3}{1-4}\right)$

$\to (-1)\left(\frac{1-4^3}{1-4}\right) = -21$

✎ *Evaluate each geometric series described.*

1) $1 + 2 + 4 + 8 \ldots, n = 6$ _____

2) $1 - 4 + 16 - 64 \ldots, n = 9$ _____

3) $-2 - 6 - 18 - 54 \ldots, n = 9$ _____

4) $2 - 10 + 50 - 250 \ldots, n = 8$ _____

5) $1 - 5 + 25 - 125 \ldots, n = 7$ _____

6) $-3 - 6 - 12 - 24 \ldots, n = 9$ _____

Infinite Geometric Series

Step-by-step guide:

✓ Infinite Geometric Series: The sum of a geometric series is infinite when the absolute value of the ratio is more than 1.
✓ Infinite Geometric Series formula: $S = \sum_{i=0}^{\infty} a_i r^i = \frac{a_1}{1-r}$

Examples:

1) **Evaluate infinite geometric series described.** $\sum_{i=1}^{\infty} 9^{i-1}$

   Use this formula: $\sum_{i=0}^{\infty} a_i r^i = \frac{a_1}{1-r} \rightarrow \sum_{i=1}^{\infty} 9^{i-1} = \frac{1}{1-9} = \frac{1}{-8} = -\frac{1}{8}$

2) **Evaluate infinite geometric series described.** $\sum_{k=1}^{\infty} (\frac{1}{4})^{k-1}$

   Use this formula: $\sum_{i=0}^{\infty} a_i r^i = \frac{a_1}{1-r} \rightarrow \sum_{k=1}^{\infty} (\frac{1}{4})^{k-1} = \frac{1}{1-\frac{1}{4}} = \frac{1}{\frac{3}{4}} = \frac{4}{3}$

✎ Determine if each geometric series converges or diverges.

1) $a_1 = -1, r = 3$

2) $a_1 = 3.2, r = 0.2$

3) $a_1 = 5, r = 2$

4) $-1, 3, -9, 27, \ldots$

5) $2, -1, \frac{1}{2}, -\frac{1}{4}, \frac{1}{8}, \ldots$

6) $81 + 27 + 9 + 3 \ldots$

✎ Evaluate each infinite geometric series described.

7) $\sum_{k=1}^{\infty} 4^{k-1}$

8) $\sum_{i=1}^{\infty} 5 \cdot (-\frac{1}{5})^{i-1}$

9) $\sum_{k=1}^{\infty} (-\frac{1}{3})^{k-1}$

10) $\sum_{n=1}^{\infty} 16(\frac{1}{4})^{n-1}$

Answers – Day 28

Finite Geometric

1) 63
2) 52,429
3) −19,682
4) −130,208
5) 13,021
6) −513

Infinite Geometric

1) Diverges
2) Converges
3) Converges
4) Diverges
5) Converges
6) Converges
7) Infinite
8) $\frac{25}{6}$
9) $\frac{3}{4}$
10) $\frac{64}{3}$

Day 29: Time to Test

CLEP College Algebra Test Review

College-Level Examination Program (CLEP) is a series of 33 standardized tests that measures your knowledge of certain subjects. You can earn college credit at thousands of colleges and universities by earning a satisfactory score on a computer-based CLEP exam.

The CLEP College Algebra measures your knowledge of math topics generally taught in a one-semester college course in algebra. It contains approximately 60 multiple choice questions to be answered in 90 minutes. Some of these questions are pretest questions that will not be scored. These 60 questions cover: basic algebraic operations; linear and quadratic equations, inequalities, and graphs; algebraic, exponential, and logarithmic functions; and miscellaneous other topics. A scientific calculator is available to students during the entire testing time.

The CLEP College Algebra exam score ranges from 20 to 80 converting to A, B, C, or D based on this score. The letter grade is applied to your college course equivalent.

On Days 29 and 30, there are two complete CLEP College Algebra Tests. Take these tests to see what score you'll be able to receive on a real CLEP College Algebra test.

Good luck!

Time to refine your quantitative reasoning skill with a practice test

Take a CLEP College Algebra test to simulate the test day experience. After you've finished, score your test using the answer keys.

Before You Start

- You'll need a pencil, a calculator and a timer to take the test.
- For most multiple questions, there are five possible answers. Choose which one is best.
- It's okay to guess. There is no penalty for wrong answers.
- Use the answer sheet provided to record your answers.
- **Calculator is permitted for CLEP College Algebra Test.**
- After you've finished the test, review the answer key to see where you went wrong.

Good Luck!

CLEP College Algebra Practice Test

2020

Total number of questions: 60

Total time: 90 Minutes

Calculator is permitted for CLEP College Algebra Test.

CLEP College Algebra Practice Test Answer Sheet

Remove (or photocopy) this answer sheet and use it to complete the practice test.

CLEP College Algebra Practice Test Answer Sheet		
1 Ⓐ Ⓑ Ⓒ Ⓓ Ⓔ	21 Ⓐ Ⓑ Ⓒ Ⓓ Ⓔ	41 Ⓐ Ⓑ Ⓒ Ⓓ Ⓔ
2 Ⓐ Ⓑ Ⓒ Ⓓ Ⓔ	22 Ⓐ Ⓑ Ⓒ Ⓓ Ⓔ	42 Ⓐ Ⓑ Ⓒ Ⓓ Ⓔ
3 Ⓐ Ⓑ Ⓒ Ⓓ Ⓔ	23 Ⓐ Ⓑ Ⓒ Ⓓ Ⓔ	43 Ⓐ Ⓑ Ⓒ Ⓓ Ⓔ
4 Ⓐ Ⓑ Ⓒ Ⓓ Ⓔ	24 Ⓐ Ⓑ Ⓒ Ⓓ Ⓔ	44 Ⓐ Ⓑ Ⓒ Ⓓ Ⓔ
5 Ⓐ Ⓑ Ⓒ Ⓓ Ⓔ	25 Ⓐ Ⓑ Ⓒ Ⓓ Ⓔ	45 Ⓐ Ⓑ Ⓒ Ⓓ Ⓔ
6 Ⓐ Ⓑ Ⓒ Ⓓ Ⓔ	26 Ⓐ Ⓑ Ⓒ Ⓓ Ⓔ	46 Ⓐ Ⓑ Ⓒ Ⓓ Ⓔ
7 Ⓐ Ⓑ Ⓒ Ⓓ Ⓔ	27 Ⓐ Ⓑ Ⓒ Ⓓ Ⓔ	47 Ⓐ Ⓑ Ⓒ Ⓓ Ⓔ
8 Ⓐ Ⓑ Ⓒ Ⓓ Ⓔ	28 Ⓐ Ⓑ Ⓒ Ⓓ Ⓔ	48 Ⓐ Ⓑ Ⓒ Ⓓ Ⓔ
9 Ⓐ Ⓑ Ⓒ Ⓓ Ⓔ	29 Ⓐ Ⓑ Ⓒ Ⓓ Ⓔ	49 Ⓐ Ⓑ Ⓒ Ⓓ Ⓔ
10 Ⓐ Ⓑ Ⓒ Ⓓ Ⓔ	30 Ⓐ Ⓑ Ⓒ Ⓓ Ⓔ	50 Ⓐ Ⓑ Ⓒ Ⓓ Ⓔ
11 Ⓐ Ⓑ Ⓒ Ⓓ Ⓔ	31 Ⓐ Ⓑ Ⓒ Ⓓ Ⓔ	51 Ⓐ Ⓑ Ⓒ Ⓓ Ⓔ
12 Ⓐ Ⓑ Ⓒ Ⓓ Ⓔ	32 Ⓐ Ⓑ Ⓒ Ⓓ Ⓔ	52 Ⓐ Ⓑ Ⓒ Ⓓ Ⓔ
13 Ⓐ Ⓑ Ⓒ Ⓓ Ⓔ	33 Ⓐ Ⓑ Ⓒ Ⓓ Ⓔ	53 Ⓐ Ⓑ Ⓒ Ⓓ Ⓔ
14 Ⓐ Ⓑ Ⓒ Ⓓ Ⓔ	34 Ⓐ Ⓑ Ⓒ Ⓓ Ⓔ	54 Ⓐ Ⓑ Ⓒ Ⓓ Ⓔ
15 Ⓐ Ⓑ Ⓒ Ⓓ Ⓔ	35 Ⓐ Ⓑ Ⓒ Ⓓ Ⓔ	55 Ⓐ Ⓑ Ⓒ Ⓓ Ⓔ
16 Ⓐ Ⓑ Ⓒ Ⓓ Ⓔ	36 Ⓐ Ⓑ Ⓒ Ⓓ Ⓔ	56 Ⓐ Ⓑ Ⓒ Ⓓ Ⓔ
17 Ⓐ Ⓑ Ⓒ Ⓓ Ⓔ	37 Ⓐ Ⓑ Ⓒ Ⓓ Ⓔ	57 Ⓐ Ⓑ Ⓒ Ⓓ Ⓔ
18 Ⓐ Ⓑ Ⓒ Ⓓ Ⓔ	38 Ⓐ Ⓑ Ⓒ Ⓓ Ⓔ	58 Ⓐ Ⓑ Ⓒ Ⓓ Ⓔ
19 Ⓐ Ⓑ Ⓒ Ⓓ Ⓔ	39 Ⓐ Ⓑ Ⓒ Ⓓ Ⓔ	59 Ⓐ Ⓑ Ⓒ Ⓓ Ⓔ
20 Ⓐ Ⓑ Ⓒ Ⓓ Ⓔ	40 Ⓐ Ⓑ Ⓒ Ⓓ Ⓔ	60 Ⓐ Ⓑ Ⓒ Ⓓ Ⓔ

1) What is the value of the expression $2(2x - y) + (4 - x)^2$ when $x = 2$ and $y = -1$?
   A. -2
   B. 8
   C. 14
   D. 28
   E. 50

2) If $x + y = 0, 4x - 2y = 24$, which of the following ordered pairs (x, y) satisfies both equations?
   A. $(4, 3)$
   B. $(5, 4)$
   C. $(4, -4)$
   D. $(4, -6)$
   E. $(2, -6)$

3) Which of the following is equivalent to $13 < -3x - 2 < 22$?
   A. $-8 < x < -5$
   B. $5 < x < 8$
   C. $\frac{11}{3} < x < \frac{20}{3}$
   D. $\frac{-20}{3} < x < \frac{-11}{3}$

4) If $f(x) = x^3 - 2x^2 + 8x$ and $g(x) = 3$, what is the value of $f(g(x))$?
   A. -3
   B. 11
   C. 22
   D. 23
   E. 33

5) The diagonal of a rectangle is 10 *inches* long and the height of the rectangle is 8 *inches*. What is the perimeter of the rectangle?
   A. 10 *inches*
   B. 12 *inches*
   C. 16 *inches*
   D. 18 *inches*
   E. 28 *inches*

Ace the CLEP College Algebra in 30 Days

6) Which of the following is an equation of a circle in the xy-plane with center $(1, 3)$ and a radius with endpoint $(5, 6)$?

   A. $(x + 1)^2 + (y + 3)^2 = \frac{61}{9}$
   B. $2x^2 + (y + 4)^2 = 25$
   C. $(x - 1)^2 + (y - 3)^2 = 5$
   D. $(x - 1)^2 + (y - 3)^2 = 25$
   E. $(x - 1)^2 + (y - 1)^2 = \frac{61}{9}$

7) The average of seven numbers is 32. If an eighth number 18 is added, then, what is the new average?
   A. 24
   B. 28
   C. 30.25
   D. 32
   E. 34

8) Given a right triangle $\triangle ABC$ whose $n\angle B = 90°$, $\sin C = \frac{2}{3}$, find $\cos A$?

   A. 1
   B. $\frac{1}{2}$
   C. $\frac{2}{3}$
   D. $\frac{3}{2}$
   E. $\frac{3}{4}$

9) What is the value of x in the following equation? $\frac{2}{3}x + \frac{1}{6} = \frac{1}{3}$

   A. 6
   B. $\frac{1}{2}$
   C. $\frac{1}{3}$
   D. $\frac{1}{4}$
   E. $\frac{1}{12}$

10) A bank is offering 2.5% simple interest on a savings account. If you deposit $16,000, how much interest will you earn in three years?
   A. $610
   B. $1,200
   C. $2,400
   D. $4,800
   E. $6,400

11) If $4n - 3 \geq 1$, what is the least possible value of $4n + 3$?
   A. 3
   B. 4
   C. 7
   D. 9
   E. 12

12) What is the ratio of the minimum value to the maximum value of the following function?
   $$f(x) = -3x + 1 \quad\quad -2 \leq x \leq 3$$
   A. $\frac{7}{8}$
   B. $-\frac{8}{7}$
   C. $-\frac{7}{8}$
   D. $\frac{8}{7}$
   E. $\frac{12}{7}$

13) The equation $x^2 = 4x - 3$ has how many distinct real solutions?
   A. 0
   B. 1
   C. 2
   D. 4
   E. 6

14) Which of the following is equal to the expression below?
   $$(3x - y)(2x + 2y)$$
   A. $6x^2 - 2y^2$
   B. $6x^2 + 4xy + 2y^2$
   C. $12x^2 + 6xy + 2y^2$
   D. $6x^2 + 4xy - 2y^2$
   E. $4x^2 + 6xy - 2y^2$

15) What is the product of all possible values of x in the following equation?

$$|x - 12| = 4$$

- A. 4
- B. 8
- C. 16
- D. 128
- E. 200

16) What is the slope of a line that is perpendicular to the line $4x - 2y = 12$?
    - A. -2
    - B. $-\frac{1}{2}$
    - C. 4
    - D. 12
    - E. 14

17) Last week 18,000 fans attended a football match. This week three times as many bought tickets, but one sixth of them cancelled their tickets. How many are attending this week?
    - A. 42,000
    - B. 54,000
    - C. 45,000
    - D. 65,000
    - E. 78,000

18) What is the perimeter of a square that has an area of 81 square inches?
    - A. $129\ inches$
    - B. $72\ inches$
    - C. $68\ inches$
    - D. $58\ inches$
    - E. $36\ inches$

19) What are the zeros of the function: $f(x) = x^2 - 7x + 12$?
    - A. 0
    - B. $-2, -3$
    - C. $0, 4, 3$
    - D. $-4, -3$
    - E. $4, 3$

20) The mean of 50 test scores was calculated as 88. But, it turned out that one of the scores was misread as 94 but it was 69. What is the mean?
   A. 85
   B. 87
   C. 87.5
   D. 88.5
   E. 90.5

21) What is the equivalent temperature of $122°F$ in Celsius?
$C = \frac{5}{9}(F - 32)$
   A. 22
   B. 50
   C. 58
   D. 62
   E. 84

22) The perimeter of a rectangular *yard* is 120 *meters*. What is its length if its width is twice its length?
   A. 20 *meters*
   B. 22 *meters*
   C. 24 *meters*
   D. 28 *meters*
   E. 30 *meters*

23) The cost of using a car is $0.35 per minutes. Which of the following equations represents the total cost c, in dollars, for h hours of using the car?
   A. $c = \frac{60h}{035}$
   B. $c = \frac{0.35}{60h}$
   C. $c = 0.35\,(60h)$
   D. $c = 60h + 0.35$
   E. $c = 60h$

24) What is the slope of the line: $8x - 4y = 8$?
   A. -1
   B. -2
   C. 1
   D. 1.5
   E. 2

$$f(x) = \frac{1}{(x-3)^2 + 4(x-3) + 4}$$

25) For what value of x is the function f(x) above undefinded?
    A. -1
    B. -2
    C. 1
    D. 1.5
    E. 2

26) The average of 8 numbers is 14. The average of 6 of those numbers is 12. What is the average of the other two numbers?
    A. 12
    B. 14
    C. 16
    D. 20
    E. 28

27) Five years ago, Amy was three times as old as Mike was. If Mike is 10 years old now, how old is Amy?
    A. 4
    B. 8
    C. 12
    D. 14
    E. 20

28) $f(a) = |12 - a^2|$, where x is a positive integer. If $f(a) = 20$, what is the value of a that satisfies the equation above?
    A. -1
    B. 0
    C. 3
    D. 4
    E. 5

29) x is $y\%$ of what number?

   A. $\dfrac{100x}{y}$

   B. $\dfrac{100y}{x}$

   C. $\dfrac{x}{100y}$

   D. $\dfrac{y}{100x}$

   E. $\dfrac{xy}{100}$

30) If cotangent of an angel β is 1, then the tangent of angle β is

   A. -1

   B. 0

   C. 1

   D. 2

   E. 3

31) The sum of four numbers is 600. One of the numbers, x is 50% more than the sum of the other three numbers. What is the value of x?

   A. 90

   B. 180

   C. 360

   D. 520

   E. 800

32) The profit in dollars from a carwash is given by the function $P(x) = \dfrac{40a-500}{a} + b$, where a is the number of cars washed and b is a constant. If 50 cars were washed today for a total profit of $600, what is the value of b?

   A. 440

   B. 570

   C. 620

   D. 910

   E. 980

33) If $|a| < 1$, then which of the following is true? $(b > 0)$?

    I. $-b < ba < b$

    II. $-a < a^2 < a$ $if\ a < 0$

    III. $-5 < 2a - 3 < -1$

- A. I only
- B. II only
- C. I and III only
- D. III only
- E. I, II and III

34) A cruise line ship left Port A and traveled 80 miles due west and then 150 miles due north. At this point, what is the shortest distance from the cruise to port A?
- A. 70 miles
- B. 80 miles
- C. 150 miles
- D. 230 miles
- E. 170 miles

35) If 30% of a number is 12, what is the number?
- A. 12
- B. 25
- C. 40
- D. 45
- E. 50

36) The system of equations below has solution (x, y). What is the value of x?

$$\frac{3}{2}y = 5$$

$$x - \frac{3}{2}y = 3$$

- A. 3
- B. 5
- C. 8
- D. 10
- E. 10

37) Which of the following is the equation of a quadratic graph with a vertex $(3, -3)$?

   A. $y = 3x^2 - 3$
   B. $y = -3x^2 + 3$
   C. $y = x^2 + 3x - 3$
   D. $y = 4(x - 3)^2 - 3$
   E. $y = 4(x + 3)^2 - 3$

38) The following table represents the value of x and function $f(x)$. Which of the following could be the equation of the function $f(x)$?

   A. $f(x) = x^2 - 5$
   B. $f(x) = x^2 - 1$
   C. $f(x) = \sqrt{x + 2}$
   D. $f(x) = \sqrt{x} + 4$
   D. $f(x) = \sqrt{x + 1} + 4$

x	$f(x)$
1	5
4	6
9	7
16	8

39) In the following equation when z is divided by 3, what is the effect on x?

$$x = \frac{8y + \frac{r}{r+1}}{\frac{6}{z}}$$

   A. x is divided by 2
   B. x is divided by 3
   C. x does not change
   D. x is multiplied by 3
   E. x is multiplied by 2

40) If $x \blacksquare y = \sqrt{x^2 + y}$, what is the value of $6 \blacksquare 28$?

   A. $\sqrt{168}$
   B. 10
   C. 8
   D. 6
   E. 4.5

41) If x is a real number, and if $x^3 + 18 = 130$, then x lies between which two consecutive integers?
- A. 1 and 2
- B. 2 and 3
- C. 3 and 4
- D. 4 and 5
- E. 5 and 6

42) If $\frac{3x}{25} = \frac{x-1}{5}$, $x =$
- A. $\frac{1}{5}$
- B. $\frac{5}{2}$
- C. 3
- D. 5
- E. 8

43) If $(x-2)^3 = 27$ which of the following could be the value of $(x-6)(x-4)$?
- A. 1
- B. 2
- C. 6
- D. -1
- E. -2

44) Simplify $(-5 + 9i)(3 + 5i)$,
- A. $6 - 2i$
- B. $60 - 2i$
- C. $6 + 2i$
- D. $-60 + 2i$
- E. $60 + 4i$

45) If function is defined as $f(x) = bx^2 + 15$, and b is a constant and $f(2) = 35$. What is the value of $f(3)$?
- A. 25
- B. 45
- C. 60
- D. 105
- E. 115

46) Find the value of y in the following system of equations?

$$3x - 4y = -20$$
$$-x + 2y = 10$$

- A. -2
- B. 2
- C. -5
- D. 5
- E. 6

47) Calculate $f(3)$ for the function $f(x) = 3x^2 - 5$.
- A. 22
- B. 30
- C. 48
- D. 50
- E. 60

48) What are the zeroes of the function $f(x) = x^3 + 8x^2 + 12x$?

- A. 2
- B. 6
- C. $0, 2, 6$
- D. $0, -2, -6$
- E. $0, -2, 6$

49) If the area of the following rectangular $ABCD$ is 100, and E is the midpoint of AB, what is the area of the shaded part
- A. 25
- B. 45
- C. 50
- D. 80
- E. 90

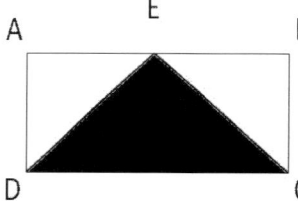

$$y = x^2 - 9x + 14$$

50) The equation above represents a parabola in the xy-plane. Which of the following equivalent forms of the equation displays the x-intercepts of the parabola as constants or coefficients?

- A. $y = x + 2$
- B. $y = x(x - 7)$
- C. $y = (x + 2)(x + 7)$
- D. $y = (x - 2)(x - 7)$
- E. $y = (x - 1)(x - 7)$

51) The function $g(x)$ is defined by a polynomial. Some values of x and $g(x)$ are shown in the table below. Which of the following must be a factor of $g(x)$?
   A. $x - 2$
   B. $x - 1$
   C. $x + 2$
   D. $x + 1$
   E. $x + 3$

x	$g(x)$
-1	4
-2	0
0	5
1	4
2	6

52) What is the value of $\frac{8b}{c}$ when $\frac{c}{b} = 2$
   A. 6
   B. 5
   C. 4
   D. 1
   E. 0

53) $\dfrac{1\frac{4}{3} + \frac{1}{4}}{2\frac{1}{2} - \frac{17}{8}}$ is approximately equal to
   A. 5.88
   B. 6.88
   C. 9
   D. 12
   E. 16

54) Which is the correct statement?
   A. $\frac{3}{4} > 0.8$
   B. $10\% = \frac{2}{5}$
   C. $3 < \frac{5}{2}$
   D. $\frac{5}{6} > 0.8$
   E. None of them above

55) Which of the following lines is parallel to: $y - 2x = 36$?
   A. $y = 2x + 2$
   B. $y = 3x + 5$
   C. $y = x - 2$
   D. $y = \frac{1}{3}x - 1$
   E. $y = -x - 1$

56) When 40% of 60 is added to 12% of 600, the resulting number is:

   A. 24
   B. 72
   C. 96
   D. 140
   E. 180

57) If $f(x) = 7x - 5$ and $g(x) = 2x^2 - 4x$, then find $(\frac{f}{g})(x)$.

   A. $\frac{7x-5}{2x^2-4x}$
   B. $\frac{x-1}{x^2-1}$
   C. $\frac{7x-1}{x^2-2}$
   D. $\frac{7x+5}{x^2+2x}$
   E. $\frac{x+5}{x^2+2x}$

58) What is the solution of the following inequality?

$$|x - 2| \geq 4$$

   A. $x \geq 6 \cup x \leq -2$
   B. $-2 \leq x \leq 6$
   C. $x \geq 6$
   D. $x \leq -2$
   E. $x \leq 2$

59) Let r and p be constants. If $x^2 + 6x + r$ factors into $(x + 2)(x + p)$, the values of r and p respectively are?

   A. 8 , 4
   B. 4 , 8
   C. 6 , 3
   D. 3 , 6
   E. 2 , 6

60) Which of the following expressions is equal to $\sqrt{\frac{x^2}{2} + \frac{x^2}{16}}$?

    A. x

    B. $\frac{3x}{4}$

    C. $x\sqrt{x}$

    D. $\frac{x\sqrt{x}}{4}$

    E. $\frac{x\sqrt{x}}{2}$

End of CLEP College Algebra Practice Test

CLEP College Algebra Practice Test

Answers Key

CLEP College Algebra Practice Test					
1	C	21	B	41	D
2	C	22	A	42	B
3	A	23	C	43	D
4	E	24	E	44	D
5	E	25	C	45	C
6	D	26	D	46	D
7	C	27	E	47	A
8	C	28	C	48	D
9	D	29	A	49	C
10	B	30	C	50	D
11	C	31	C	51	C
12	B	32	B	52	C
13	C	33	C	53	B
14	D	34	E	54	D
15	D	35	C	55	A
16	B	36	C	56	C
17	C	37	D	57	A
18	E	38	D	58	A
19	E	39	B	59	A
20	C	40	C	60	B

CLEP College Algebra Practice Test

Answers and Explanations

✱ Now, it's time to review your results to see where you went wrong and what areas you need to improve.

1) Choice C is correct

Plug in the value of x and y: $x = 2$ and $y = -1$

$2(2x - y) + (4 - x)^2 = x^2 - 4x - 2y + 16 = (2)^2 - 4(2) - 2(-1) + 16 = 14$

2) Choice C is correct

Plugin the values of x and y provided in the options into both equations.

A. $(4, 3)$ $x + y = 0 \rightarrow 4 + 3 \neq 0$
B. $(5, 4)$ $x + y = 0 \rightarrow 5 + 4 \neq 0$
C. $(4, -4)$ $x + y = 0 \rightarrow 4 + (-4) = 0$
D. $(4, -6)$ $x + y = 0 \rightarrow 4 + (-6) \neq 0$
E. $(2, -6)$ $x + y = 0 \rightarrow 2 + (-6) \neq 0$

Only choice C is correct.

3) Choice A is correct

$13 < -3x - 2 < 22 \rightarrow$ Add 2 to all sides. $13 + 2 < -3x - 2 + 2 < 22 + 2$

$\rightarrow 15 < -3x < 24 \rightarrow$ Divide all sides by -3. (Remember that when you divide all sides of an inequality by a negative number, the inequality sing will be swapped. < becomes >)

$\frac{15}{-3} > \frac{-3x}{-3} > \frac{24}{-3}.$ $-8 < x < -5$

4) Choice E is correct

$g(x) = 3$, then $f(g(x)) = f(3) = (3)^3 - 2(3)^2 + 8(3) = 27 - 18 + 24 = 33$

5) Choice E is correct

Let x be the width of the rectangle. Use Pythagorean Theorem:

$a^2 + b^2 = c^2$

$x^2 + 8^2 = 10^2 \Rightarrow x^2 + 64 = 100 \Rightarrow x^2 = 100 - 64 = 36 \Rightarrow x = 6$

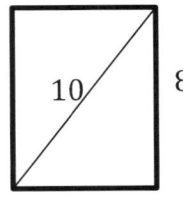

Perimeter of the rectangle $= 2(length + width) = 2(8 + 6) = 2(14) = 28$

6) Choice D is correct

The equation of a circle can be written as $(x - h)^2 + (y - k)^2 = r^2$

where (h, k) are the coordinates of the center of the circle and r is the radius of the circle. Since the coordinates of the center of the circle are $(1, 3)$, the equation is

$(x-1)^2 + (y-3)^2 = r^2$, where r is the radius. The radius of the circle is the distance from the center (1, 3), to the given endpoint of a radius, (5, 6). By the distance formula, $r^2 = (5-1)^2 + (6-3)^2 = 16 + 9 = 25$

Therefore, an equation of the given circle is $(x-1)^2 + (y-3)^2 = 25$

7) Choice C is correct

Solve for the sum of seven numbers: $average = \frac{sum\ of\ terms}{number\ of\ terms} \Rightarrow 32 = \frac{sum\ of\ 7\ numbers}{7} \Rightarrow$ $sum\ of\ 7\ numbers = 32 \times 7 = 224$, The sum of 7 numbers is 224. If a eighth number 18 is added, then the sum of 8 numbers is :

$224 + 18 = 242$, $average = \frac{sum\ of\ terms}{number\ of\ terms} = \frac{242}{8} = 30.25$

8) Choice C is correct

To solve for $\cos A$ first identify what is known. The question states that $\triangle ABC$ is a right triangle whose $n \angle B = 90°$ and $\sin C = \frac{2}{3}$. It is important to recall that any triangle has a sum of interior angles that equals 180 degrees. Therefore, to calculate $\cos A$ use the complimentary angles identify of trigonometric function. $\cos A = \cos(90 - C)$, Then: $\cos A = \sin C$

For complementary angles, sin of one angle is equal to cos of the other angle. $\cos A = \frac{2}{3}$

9) Choice D is correct

Isolate and solve for x: $\frac{2}{3}x + \frac{1}{6} = \frac{1}{3} \Rightarrow \frac{2}{3}x = \frac{1}{3} - \frac{1}{6} = \frac{1}{6} \Rightarrow \frac{2}{3}x = \frac{1}{6}$

Multiply both sides by the reciprocal of the coefficient of x.

$(\frac{3}{2})\frac{2}{3}x = \frac{1}{6}(\frac{3}{2}) \Rightarrow x = \frac{3}{12} = \frac{1}{4}$

10) Choice B is correct

Use simple interest formula: $I = prt$, ($I = interest, p = principal, r = rate, t = time$)

$I = (16,000)(0.025)(3) = 1,200$

11) Choice C is correct

Adding 6 to each side of the inequality $4n - 3 \geq 1$ yields the inequality $4n + 3 \geq 7$. Therefore, the least possible value of $4n + 3$ is 7.

12) Choice B is correct

Since $f(x)$ is linear function with a negative slop, then when $x = -2$, $f(x)$ is maximum and when $x = 3$, $f(x)$ is minimum. Then the ratio of the minimum value to the maximum value of the function is: $\frac{f(3)}{f(-2)} = \frac{-3(3)+1}{-3(-2)+1} = \frac{-8}{7} = -\frac{8}{7}$

13) Choice C is correct

There can be 0, 1, or 2 solutions to a quadratic equation. In standard form, a quadratic equation is written as: $ax^2 + bx + c = 0$. For the quadratic equation, the expression $b^2 - 4ac$ is called discriminant. If discriminant is positive, there are 2 distinct solutions for the quadratic equation. If discriminant is 0, there is one solution for the quadratic equation and if it is negative the equation does not have any solutions. To find number of solutions for $x^2 = 4x - 3$, first, rewrite it as $x^2 - 4x + 3 = 0$. Find the value of the discriminant. $b^2 - 4ac = (-4)^2 - 4(1)(3) = 16 - 12 = 4$.

Since the discriminant is positive, the quadratic equation has two distinct solutions.

14) Choice D is correct

Use FOIL method: $(3x - y)(2x + 2y) = 6x^2 + 6xy - 2xy - 2y^2 = 6x^2 + 4xy - 2y^2$

15) Choice D is correct

To solve absolute values equations, write two equations. $x - 12$ could be positive 4, or negative -4. Therefore, $x - 12 = 4 \Rightarrow x = 16$, $x - 12 = -4 \Rightarrow x = 8$. Find the product of solutions: $8 \times 16 = 128$

16) Choice B is correct

The equation of a line in slope intercept form is: $y = mx + b$

Solve for y: $4x - 2y = 12 \Rightarrow -2y = 12 - 4x \Rightarrow y = (12 - 4x) \div (-2) \Rightarrow$

$y = 2x - 6$, The slope is 2, The slope of the line perpendicular to this line is:

$m_1 \times m_2 = -1 \Rightarrow 2 \times m_2 = -1 \Rightarrow m_2 = -\frac{1}{2}$

17) Choice C is correct

Three times of 18,000 is 54,000. One sixth of them cancelled their tickets.

One sixth of 54,000 equals 9,000 ($\frac{1}{6} \times 54,000 = 9,000$).

45,000 ($54,000 - 9,000 = 45,000$) fans are attending this week.

18) Choice E is correct

The area of the square is 81 inches. Therefore, the side of the square is square root of the area. $\sqrt{81} = 9$ inches. Four times the side of the square is the perimeter: $4 \times 9 = 36\ inches$

19) Choice E is correct

First factor the function: $(x - 4)(x - 3)$. To find the zeros, $f(x)$ should be zero: $f(x) = (x - 4)(x - 3) = 0$, Therefore, the zeros are, $(x - 4) = 0 \Rightarrow x = 4$, $(x - 3) = 0 \Rightarrow x = 3$

20) Choice C is correct

$average\ (mean) = \dfrac{sum\ of\ terms}{number\ of\ terms} \Rightarrow 88 = \dfrac{sum\ of\ terms}{50} \Rightarrow sum = 88 \times 50 = 4400$

The difference of 94 and 69 is 25. Therefore, 25 should be subtracted from the sum.

$$4400 - 25 = 4375, mean = \frac{sum\ of\ terms}{number\ of\ terms} \Rightarrow mean = \frac{4375}{50} = 87.5$$

21) Choice B is correct

Plug in 122 for F and then solve for C.

$$C = \frac{5}{9}(F - 32) \Rightarrow C = \frac{5}{9}(122 - 32) \Rightarrow C = \frac{5}{9}(90) = 50$$

22) Choice A is correct

The width of the rectangle is twice its length. Let x be the length. Then, $width = 2x$

Perimeter of the rectangle is: $2\ (width + length) = 2(2x + x) = 120 \Rightarrow 6x = 120 \Rightarrow x = 20$. Length of the rectangle is 20 meters.

23) Choice C is correct

$0.35 per minute to use car. This per-minute rate can be converted to the hourly rate using the conversion 1 hour = 60 minutes, as shown below.

$$\frac{0.35}{minute} \times \frac{60\ minutes}{1\ hours} = \frac{\$(0.35 \times 60)}{hour}$$

Thus, the car costs (0.35×60) per hour.

Therefore, the cost c, in dollars, for h hours of use is $c = (0.35 \times 60)h$,

Which is equivalent to $c = 0.35(60h)$

24) Choice E is correct

Solve for y: $8x - 4y = 8$, Divided both sides by -4: $\frac{8}{-4}x - \frac{4}{-4}y = \frac{8}{-4}$

$-2x + y = -2 \rightarrow y = 2x - 2$, Then: The slope of the line is 2.

25) Choice C is correct

The function $f(x)$ is undefined when the denominator of $\frac{1}{(x-3)^2+4(x-3)+4}$ is equal to zero. The expression $(x - 3)^2 + 4(x - 3) + 4$ is a perfect square.

$(x - 3)^2 + 4(x - 3) + 4 = ((x - 3) + 2)^2$ which can be rewritten as $(x - 1)^2$. The expression $(x - 1)^2$ is equal to zero if and only if $x = 1$. Therefore, the value of x for which $f(x)$ is undefined is 1.

26) Choice D is correct

$average = \frac{sum\ of\ terms}{number\ of\ terms} \Rightarrow$ (average of 8 numbers) $14 = \frac{sum\ of\ numbers}{8} \Rightarrow$ sum of 8 numbers is: $14 \times 8 = 112$

(average of 6 numbers) $12 = \frac{sum\ of\ numbers}{6} \Rightarrow$ sum of 6 numbers is: $12 \times 6 = 72$

$sum\ of\ 8\ numbers - sum\ of\ 6\ numbers = sum\ of\ 2\ numbers$

$112 - 72 = 40 \quad$ average of 2 numbers $= \frac{40}{2} = 20$

27) Choice E is correct

Five years ago, Amy was three times as old as Mike. Mike is 10 years now. Therefore, 5 years ago Mike was 5 years. Five years ago, Amy was: $A = 3 \times 5 = 15$, Now Amy is 20 years old: $15 + 5 = 20$

28) Choice C is correct

Since we are dealing with an absolute value, $f(a) = 20$ means that either $11 - a^2 = 20$ or $11 - a^2 = -20$. Let's start with the positive value (20) and see what we get. If $11 - a^2 = 20$, then $a^2 = 9$. Taking the square root, we get $a = 3 \text{ or} -3$, On the other hand, if $11 - a^2 = -20$, then: $a = \sqrt{-31}$, Notice that the question states that a is a positive integer, therefore the answer is 3.

29) Choice A is correct.

Let the number be A. Then: $x = y\% \times A$. Solve for A. $x = \frac{y}{100} \times A$

Multiply both sides by $\frac{100}{y}$: $x \times \frac{100}{y} = \frac{y}{100} \times \frac{100}{y} \times A \rightarrow A = \frac{100x}{y}$

30) Choice C is correct

$$tangent \ \beta = \frac{1}{cotangent \ \beta} = \frac{1}{1} = 1$$

31) Choice C is correct

One of the four numbers is x; let the other three numbers be y, z and w. Since the sum of four numbers is 600, the equation $x + y + z + w = 600$ is true. The statement that x is 50% more than the sum of the other three numbers can be represented as

$$x = 1.5(y + z + w) \text{ or } \frac{x}{1.5} = y + z + w \rightarrow \frac{2x}{3} = y + z + w$$

Substituting the value $y + z + w$ in the equation $x + y + z + w = 600$

gives $x + \frac{2x}{3} = 600 \rightarrow \frac{5x}{3} = 600 \rightarrow 5x = 1{,}800 \rightarrow x = \frac{1{,}800}{5} = 360$

32) Choice B is correct

This is a simple matter of substituting values for variables.

We are given that the 50 cars were washed today, therefore we can substitute that for a.

Giving us the expression $\frac{40(50)-500}{50} + b$. We are also given that the profit was $600, which we can substitute for $f(a)$. Which gives us the equation $600 = \frac{40(50)-500}{50} + b$

Simplifying the fraction gives us the equation $600 = 30 + b$

And subtracting both sides of the equation by 30 gives us $b = 570$, which is the answer.

33) Choice C is correct

I. $|a| < 1 \rightarrow -1 < a < 1$

Multiply all sides by b. Since, $b > 0 \rightarrow -b < ba < b$ (it is true!)

II. Since, $-1 < a < 1$, and $a < 0 \rightarrow -a > a^2 > a$ (plug in $-\frac{1}{2}$, and check!) (It's false)

III. $-1 < a < 1$, multiply all sides by 2, then: $-2 < 2a < 2$

Subtract 3 from all sides. Then: $-2 - 3 < 2a - 3 < 2 - 3 \rightarrow -5 < 2a - 3 < -1$ (It is true!)

34) Choice E is correct

Use Pythagorean Theorem: $a^2 + b^2 = c^2$

$80^2 + 150^2 = c^2 \Rightarrow 6400 + 22500 = c^2 \Rightarrow 28900 = c^2 \Rightarrow c = 170$

35) Choice C is correct

Let x be the number. Write the equation and solve for x.

$30\%\ of\ x = 12 \Rightarrow 0.30x = 12 \Rightarrow x = 12 \div 0.30 = 40$

36) Choice C is correct

Adding the two equations side by side eliminates y and yields $x = 8$.

$\frac{3}{2}y = 5, \quad x - \frac{3}{2}y = 3, \quad \rightarrow x + 0 = 8 \rightarrow x = 8$

37) Choice D is correct

Let's find the vertex of each choice provided:

A. $y = 3x^2 - 3$ The vertex is: $(0, -3)$
B. $y = -3x^2 + 3$ The vertex is: $(0, 3)$
C. $y = x^2 + 3x - 3$

The value of x of the vertex in the equation of a quadratic in standard form is: $x = \frac{-b}{2a} = \frac{-3}{2}$
(The standard equation of a quadratic is: $ax^2 + bx + c = 0$)
The value of x in the vertex is 3 not $\frac{-3}{2}$.

D. $y = 4(x - 3)^2 - 3$

Vertex form of a parabola equation is in form of $y = a(x - h)^2 + k$, where (h, k) is the vertex. Then $h = 3$ and $k = -3$. (This is the answer)

E. $y = 4(x+3)^2 - 3$ The vertex in this equation is $(-3, -3)$.

38) Choice D is correct

A. $f(x) = x^2 - 5$ if $x = 1 \to f(1) = (1)^2 - 5 = 1 - 5 = -4 \neq 5$

B. $f(x) = x^2 - 1$ if $x = 1 \to f(1) = (1)^2 - 1 = 1 - 1 = 0 \neq 5$

C. $f(x) = \sqrt{x+2}$ if $x = 1 \to f(1) = \sqrt{1+2} = \sqrt{3} \neq 5$

D. $f(x) = \sqrt{x} + 4$ if $x = 1 \to f(1) = \sqrt{1} + 4 = 5$

E. $f(x) = \sqrt{x+1} + 4$ if $x = 1 \to f(1) = \sqrt{1+1} + 4 \neq 5$

39) Choice B is correct

Plug in $z/3$ for z and simplify.

$$x_1 = \frac{8y + \frac{r}{r+1}}{\frac{6}{\frac{z}{3}}} = \frac{8y + \frac{r}{r+1}}{\frac{3 \times 6}{z}} = \frac{8y + \frac{r}{r+1}}{3 \times \frac{6}{z}} = \frac{1}{3} \times \frac{8y + \frac{r}{r+1}}{\frac{6}{z}} = \frac{x}{3}$$

40) Choice C is correct

Substitute x by 6 and y by 28 in the equation. Then:

$6 \blacksquare 28 = \sqrt{6^2 + 28} = \sqrt{36 + 28} = \sqrt{64} = 8$

41) Choice D is correct

Solve for x: $x^3 + 18 = 130 \to x^3 = 112$
Let's review the choices.
A. 1 and 2. $1^3 = 1$ and $2^3 = 8$, 112 is not between these two numbers.
B. 2 and 3. $2^3 = 8$ and $3^3 = 27$, 112 is not between these two numbers.
C. 3 and 4. $3^3 = 27$ and $4^3 = 64$, 112 is not between these two numbers.
D. 4 and 5. $4^3 = 64$ and $5^3 = 125$, 112 is between these two numbers.
E. 5 and 6. $5^3 = 125$ and $6^3 = 126$, 112 is not between these two numbers.

42) Choice B is correct.

Solve for x: $\frac{3x}{25} = \frac{x-1}{5}$, Multiply the second fraction by 5: $\frac{3x}{25} = \frac{5(x-1)}{5 \times 5}$
Tow denominators are equal. Therefore, the numerators must be equal.
$3x = 5x - 5 \to -2x = -5 \to \frac{5}{2} = x$

43) Choice D is correct

$(x-2)^3 = 27 \to x - 2 = 3 \to x = 5. \to (x-6)(x-4) = (5-6)(5-4) = (-1)(1) = -1$

44) Choice D is correct

We know that: $i = \sqrt{-1} \Rightarrow i^2 = -1$

$(-5 + 9i)(3 + 5i) = -15 - 25i + 27i + 45i^2 = -15 + 2i - 45 = 2i - 60 = -60 + 2i$

45) Choice C is correct

First find the value of b, and then find $f(3)$. Since $f(2) = 35$, substuting 2 for x and 35 for $f(x)$ gives $35 = b(2)^2 + 15 = 4b + 15$. Solving this equation gives $b = 5$. Thus

$f(x) = 5x^2 + 15, \quad f(3) = 5(3)^2 + 15 \to f(3) = 45 + 15, \quad f(3) = 60$

46) Choice D is correct

Solve the system of equations by elimination method.

$3x - 4y = -20$
$-x + 2y = 10$ Multiply the second equation by 3, then add it to the first equation.

$\begin{array}{l} 3x - 4y = -20 \\ 3(-x + 2y = 10) \end{array} \Rightarrow \begin{array}{l} 3x - 4y = -20 \\ -3x + 6y = 30) \end{array} \Rightarrow$ add the equations $2y = 10 \Rightarrow y = 5$

47) Choice A is correct

Identify the input value. Since the function is in the form $f(x)$ and the question asks to calculate $f(3)$, the input value is four. $f(3) \to x = 3$ Using the function, input the desired x value.

Now substitute 4 in for every x in the function. $f(x) = 3x^2 - 5, \quad f(3) = 3(3)^2 - 5,$

$f(3) = 27 - 5, \quad f(3) = 22$

48) Choice D is correct

Frist factor the function: $f(x) = x^3 + 8x^2 + 12x = x(x + 2)(x + 6)$, To find the zeros, $f(x)$ should be zero. $f(x) = x(x + 2)(x + 6) = 0$, Therefore, the zeros are: $x = 0, \quad (x + 2) = 0 \Rightarrow x = -2, (x + 6) = 0 \Rightarrow x = -6$

49) Choice C is correct

Since, E is the midpoint of AB, then the area of all triangles DAE, DEF, CFE and CBE are equal. Let x be the area of one of the triangle, then: $4x = 100 \to x = 25$

The area of $DEC = 2x = 2(25) = 50$

50) Choice D is correct

The x-intercepts of the parabola represented by $y = x^2 - 9x + 14$ in the xy-plane are the values of x for which y is equal to 0. The factored form of the equation, $y = (x - 2)(x - 7)$, shows that y equals 0 if and only if $x = 2$ or $x = 7$. Thus, the factored form $y = (x - 2)(x - 7)$, displays the x-intercepts of the parabola as the constants 2 and 7.

51) Choice C is correct

If $x - a$ is a factor of $g(x)$, then $g(a)$ must equal 0. Based on the table $g(-2) = 0$. Therefore, $x - (-2)$ or $x + 2$ must be a factor of $g(x)$.

52) Choice C is correct

To solve this problem first solve the equation for c. $\dfrac{c}{b} = 2$

Multiply by b on both sides. Then: $b \times \frac{c}{b} = 2 \times b \to c = 2b$. Now to calculate $\frac{8b}{c}$, substitute the value for c into the denominator and simplify. $\frac{8b}{c} = \frac{8b}{2b} = \frac{8}{2} = 4$

53) Choice B is correct

$\frac{1\frac{4}{3}+\frac{1}{4}}{2\frac{1}{2}-\frac{17}{8}} = \frac{\frac{7}{3}+\frac{1}{4}}{\frac{5}{2}-\frac{17}{8}} = \frac{\frac{28+3}{12}}{\frac{20-17}{8}} = \frac{\frac{31}{12}}{\frac{3}{8}} = \frac{31 \times 8}{12 \times 3} = \frac{31 \times 2}{3 \times 3} = \frac{62}{9} \cong 6.88$

54) Choice D is correct

Check each choice.

A. $\frac{3}{4} > 0.8$ $\frac{3}{4} = 0.75$ and it is less than 0.8. Not true!

B. $10\% = \frac{2}{5}$ $10\% = \frac{1}{10} < \frac{2}{5}$. Not True!

C. $3 < \frac{5}{2}$ $\frac{5}{2} = 2.5 < 3$. Not True!

D. $\frac{5}{6} > 0.8$ $\frac{5}{6} = 0.8333 \ldots$ and it is greater than 0.8. Bingo!

E. None of them above   Not True!

55) Choice A is correct

First write the equation in slope intercept form. Add $2x$ to both sides to get $y = 2x + 36$. The slope of this line is 2, so any line that also has a slope of 2 would be parallel to it. Only choice A has a slope of 2.

56) Choice C is correct

40% of 60 equals to: $0.40 \times 60 = 24$. 12% of 600 equals to: $0.12 \times 600 = 72$

40% of 60 is added to 12% of 600: $24 + 72 = 96$

57) Choice A is correct

$\left(\frac{f}{g}\right)(x) = \frac{f(x)}{g(x)} = \frac{7x - 5}{2x^2 - 4x}$

58) Choice A is correct

$|x - 2| \geq 4$. Then: $x - 2 \geq 4$ or $x - 2 \leq 4$. Solve both inequalities: $x - 2 \geq 4 \to x \geq 6$ and $x - 2 \leq 4 \to x \leq 6$. The solution of the inequality $|x - 2| \geq 4$ is $x \geq 6 \cup x \leq -2$

59) Choice A is correct

$(x + 2)(x + p) = x^2 + (2 + p)x + 2p \to 2 + p = 6 \to p = 4$ and $r = 2p = 8$

60) Choice B is correct.

Simplify the expression. $\sqrt{\frac{x^2}{2} + \frac{x^2}{16}} = \sqrt{\frac{8x^2}{16} + \frac{x^2}{16}} = \sqrt{\frac{9x^2}{16}} = \sqrt{\frac{9}{16}x^2} = \sqrt{\frac{9}{16}} \times \sqrt{x^2} = \frac{3}{4} \times x = \frac{3x}{4}$

Day 30: A Realistic CLEP College Algebra Test

Time to experience a REAL CLEP College Algebra Test

Take the following practice CLEP College Algebra Test to simulate the test day experience. After you've finished, score your test using the answer key.

Before You Start

- Keep your practice test experience as realistic as possible.
- You'll need a pencil, calculator, and a timer to take the test.
- It's okay to guess. You won't lose any points if you're wrong.
- After you've finished the test, review the answer key to see where you went wrong.
- **Keep Strict Timing on the Test Section!**

Good Luck!

Mathematics is not only real, but it is the only reality. ~ *Martin Gardner*

CLEP College Algebra Practice Test

2020

Total number of questions: 60

Total time: 90 Minutes

Calculator is permitted for CLEP College Algebra Test.

CLEP College Algebra Practice Test Answer Sheet

Remove (or photocopy) this answer sheet and use it to complete the practice test.

CLEP College Algebra Practice Test Answer Sheet

#		#		#	
1	Ⓐ Ⓑ Ⓒ Ⓓ Ⓔ	21	Ⓐ Ⓑ Ⓒ Ⓓ Ⓔ	41	Ⓐ Ⓑ Ⓒ Ⓓ Ⓔ
2	Ⓐ Ⓑ Ⓒ Ⓓ Ⓔ	22	Ⓐ Ⓑ Ⓒ Ⓓ Ⓔ	42	Ⓐ Ⓑ Ⓒ Ⓓ Ⓔ
3	Ⓐ Ⓑ Ⓒ Ⓓ Ⓔ	23	Ⓐ Ⓑ Ⓒ Ⓓ Ⓔ	43	Ⓐ Ⓑ Ⓒ Ⓓ Ⓔ
4	Ⓐ Ⓑ Ⓒ Ⓓ Ⓔ	24	Ⓐ Ⓑ Ⓒ Ⓓ Ⓔ	44	Ⓐ Ⓑ Ⓒ Ⓓ Ⓔ
5	Ⓐ Ⓑ Ⓒ Ⓓ Ⓔ	25	Ⓐ Ⓑ Ⓒ Ⓓ Ⓔ	45	Ⓐ Ⓑ Ⓒ Ⓓ Ⓔ
6	Ⓐ Ⓑ Ⓒ Ⓓ Ⓔ	26	Ⓐ Ⓑ Ⓒ Ⓓ Ⓔ	46	Ⓐ Ⓑ Ⓒ Ⓓ Ⓔ
7	Ⓐ Ⓑ Ⓒ Ⓓ Ⓔ	27	Ⓐ Ⓑ Ⓒ Ⓓ Ⓔ	47	Ⓐ Ⓑ Ⓒ Ⓓ Ⓔ
8	Ⓐ Ⓑ Ⓒ Ⓓ Ⓔ	28	Ⓐ Ⓑ Ⓒ Ⓓ Ⓔ	48	Ⓐ Ⓑ Ⓒ Ⓓ Ⓔ
9	Ⓐ Ⓑ Ⓒ Ⓓ Ⓔ	29	Ⓐ Ⓑ Ⓒ Ⓓ Ⓔ	49	Ⓐ Ⓑ Ⓒ Ⓓ Ⓔ
10	Ⓐ Ⓑ Ⓒ Ⓓ Ⓔ	30	Ⓐ Ⓑ Ⓒ Ⓓ Ⓔ	50	Ⓐ Ⓑ Ⓒ Ⓓ Ⓔ
11	Ⓐ Ⓑ Ⓒ Ⓓ Ⓔ	31	Ⓐ Ⓑ Ⓒ Ⓓ Ⓔ	51	Ⓐ Ⓑ Ⓒ Ⓓ Ⓔ
12	Ⓐ Ⓑ Ⓒ Ⓓ Ⓔ	32	Ⓐ Ⓑ Ⓒ Ⓓ Ⓔ	52	Ⓐ Ⓑ Ⓒ Ⓓ Ⓔ
13	Ⓐ Ⓑ Ⓒ Ⓓ Ⓔ	33	Ⓐ Ⓑ Ⓒ Ⓓ Ⓔ	53	Ⓐ Ⓑ Ⓒ Ⓓ Ⓔ
14	Ⓐ Ⓑ Ⓒ Ⓓ Ⓔ	34	Ⓐ Ⓑ Ⓒ Ⓓ Ⓔ	54	Ⓐ Ⓑ Ⓒ Ⓓ Ⓔ
15	Ⓐ Ⓑ Ⓒ Ⓓ Ⓔ	35	Ⓐ Ⓑ Ⓒ Ⓓ Ⓔ	55	Ⓐ Ⓑ Ⓒ Ⓓ Ⓔ
16	Ⓐ Ⓑ Ⓒ Ⓓ Ⓔ	36	Ⓐ Ⓑ Ⓒ Ⓓ Ⓔ	56	Ⓐ Ⓑ Ⓒ Ⓓ Ⓔ
17	Ⓐ Ⓑ Ⓒ Ⓓ Ⓔ	37	Ⓐ Ⓑ Ⓒ Ⓓ Ⓔ	57	Ⓐ Ⓑ Ⓒ Ⓓ Ⓔ
18	Ⓐ Ⓑ Ⓒ Ⓓ Ⓔ	38	Ⓐ Ⓑ Ⓒ Ⓓ Ⓔ	58	Ⓐ Ⓑ Ⓒ Ⓓ Ⓔ
19	Ⓐ Ⓑ Ⓒ Ⓓ Ⓔ	39	Ⓐ Ⓑ Ⓒ Ⓓ Ⓔ	59	Ⓐ Ⓑ Ⓒ Ⓓ Ⓔ
20	Ⓐ Ⓑ Ⓒ Ⓓ Ⓔ	40	Ⓐ Ⓑ Ⓒ Ⓓ Ⓔ	60	Ⓐ Ⓑ Ⓒ Ⓓ Ⓔ

1) Which of the following points lies on the line $2x + 4y = 6$?
   A. (2, 1)
   B. (−1, 2)
   C. (−2, 2)
   D. (2, 2)
   E. (2, 8)

2) Point A lies on the line with equation $y - 3 = 2(x + 5)$. If the x-coordinate of A is 8, what is the y-coordinate of A?

   A. 14
   B. 16
   C. 22
   D. 29
   E. 31

3) Right triangle ABC has two legs of lengths $5\ cm$ (AB) and $12\ cm$ (AC). What is the length of the third side (BC)?
   A. $4\ cm$
   B. $6\ cm$
   C. $8\ cm$
   D. $13\ cm$
   E. $20\ cm$

4) The ratio of boys to girls in a school is $2:3$. If there are 500 students in a school, how many boys are in the school?
   A. 540
   B. 360
   C. 300
   D. 280
   E. 200

5) $(7x + 2y)(5x + 2y) = ?$
   A. $2x^2 + 14xy + 2y^2$
   B. $2x^2 + 4xy + 2y^2$
   C. $7x^2 + 14xy + y^2$
   D. $10x^2 + 14xy + 4y$
   E. $35x^2 + 24xy + 4y^2$

6) Which of the following expressions is equivalent to $5x(4+2y)$?
   A. $x + 10xy$
   B. $5x + 5xy$
   C. $20xy + 2xy$
   D. $20x + 5xy$
   E. $20x + 10xy$

7) If $y = 5ab + 3b^3$, what is y when $a = 2$ and $b = 3$?
   A. 24
   B. 31
   C. 36
   D. 51
   E. 111

8) From the figure, which of the following must be true? (figure not drawn to scale)

   A. $y = z$
   B. $y = 5x$
   C. $y \geq x$
   D. $y + 4x = z$
   E. $y > x$

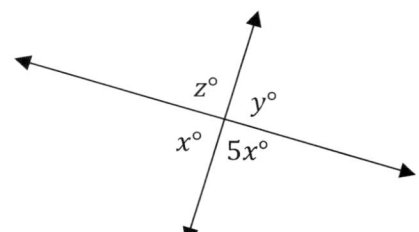

9) What is the solution of the following inequality?

   $$|x - 10| \leq 3$$

   A. $x \geq 13 \cup x \leq 7$
   B. $7 \leq x \leq 13$
   C. $x \geq 13$
   D. $x \leq 7$
   E. Set of real numbers

10) Two third of 15 is equal to $\frac{2}{5}$ of what number?
    A. 12
    B. 20
    C. 25
    D. 60
    E. 90

Ace the CLEP College Algebra in 30 Days

11) The marked price of a computer is D dollar. Its price decreased by 25% in January and later increased by 10% in February. What is the final price of the computer in D dollar?
   A. $0.80\ D$
   B. $0.82\ D$
   C. $0.90\ D$
   D. $1.20\ D$
   E. $1.40\ D$

12) If $A = \{2, 5, 11, 15\}$, $B = \{1, 2, 3, 4, 5, 6\}$, and $C = \{5, 7, 9, 11, 13\}$, then which of the following set is $(A \cup B) \cap C$?
   E. $\{1, 2, 3, 4, 5, 6, 11, 15\}$
   F. $\{1, 2, 3, 4, 5, 6, 7, 11, 13, 15\}$
   G. $\{5, 11, 13, 15\}$
   H. $\{5, 11\}$
   I. $\{11\}$

13) The average of 13, 15, 20 and x is 20. What is the value of x?
   A. 9
   B. 15
   C. 18
   D. 20
   E. 32

14) What is the ratio of the minimum value to the maximum value of the following function?
   $f(x) = -3x + 1 \qquad -2 \leq x \leq 3$
   A. $\frac{7}{8}$
   B. $-\frac{8}{7}$
   C. $-\frac{7}{8}$
   D. $\frac{8}{7}$
   E. $\frac{6}{7}$

15) The equation $x^2 = 4x - 3$ has how many distinct real solutions?
   A. 0
   B. 1
   C. 2
   D. 3
   E. 4

16) For what value of x is $|x - 3| + 3$ equal to 0?

A. 1
B. 2
C. no value of x
D. -3
E. 3

17) In 1999, the average worker's income increased $2,000 per year starting from $26,000 annual salary. Which equation represents income greater than average? (I = income, x = number of years after 1999)
    A. $I > 2000\,x + 26000$
    B. $I > -2000\,x + 26000$
    C. $I < -2000\,x + 26000$
    D. $I < 2000\,x - 26000$
    E. $I < 24{,}000\,x + 26000$

18) A boat sails 60 miles south and then 80 miles east. How far is the boat from its start point?
    A. $45\ miles$
    B. $50\ miles$
    C. $60\ miles$
    D. $70\ miles$
    E. $100\ miles$

19) In the triangle below, if the measure of angle A is 37 degrees, then what is the value of y? (figure is NOT drawn to scale)
    A. 70
    B. 78
    C. 84
    D. 86
    E. 92

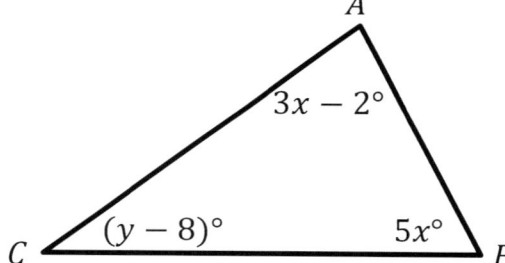

20) The score of Emma was half as that of Ava and the score of Mia was twice that of Ava. If the score of Mia was 40, what is the score of Emma?
    A. 10
    B. 15
    C. 20
    D. 30
    E. 40

21) If $A = \{1, 2, 4, 8, 16, 24\}$ and $B = \{1, 4, 12, 24, 32, 48\}$, how many elements are in $A \cup B$?
   A. 2
   B. 3
   C. 6
   D. 9
   E. 12

22) The average of five consecutive numbers is 36. What is the smallest number?
   A. 38
   B. 36
   C. 34
   D. 12
   E. 8

23) Which of the following numbers is NOT a solution of the inequality $2x - 5 \geq 3x - 1$?
   A. -2
   B. -4
   C. -5
   D. -8
   E. -10

24) If the following equations are true, what is the value of x?
$$a = \sqrt{3}$$
$$4a = \sqrt{4x}$$
   A. 2
   B. 3
   C. 6
   D. 12
   E. 14

25) If $\sqrt{4m - 3} = m$, what is (are) the value(s) of m?
   A. 0
   B. 1
   C. 1, 3
   D. $-1, 3$
   E. $-1, -3$

26) When a number is subtracted from 28 and the difference is divided by that number, the result is 3. What is the value of the number?
   A. 2
   B. 4
   C. 7
   D. 12
   E. 24

27) An angle is equal to one ninth of its supplement. What is the measure of that angle?
   A. 9
   B. 18
   C. 25
   D. 60
   E. 90

28) If $\sqrt{4m-3} = m$, what is (are) the value(s) of m?
   A. 0
   B. 1
   C. 1, 3
   D. $-1, 3$
   E. $-1, -3$

29) If $tan\ θ = \frac{5}{12}$ and $sin\ θ > 0$, then $cos\ θ = ?$
   A. $-\frac{5}{13}$
   B. $\frac{12}{13}$
   C. $\frac{13}{12}$
   D. $-\frac{12}{13}$
   E. 0

30) Which of the following has the same period and two times the amplitude of graph $y = cos\ x$?

   A. $y = cos\ 2x$
   B. $y = cos\ (x + 2)$
   C. $y = 4 cos\ 2x$
   D. $y = 2 + 2\ cos\ x$
   E. $y = 4 + cos\ x$

31) If $y = nx + 2$, where n is a constant, and when $x = 6$, $y = 14$, what is the value of y when $x = 10$?

   A. 10
   B. 12
   C. 18
   D. 22
   E. 24

32) A chemical solution contains 6% alcohol. If there is 24 ml of alcohol, what is the volume of the solution?
   A. 240 ml
   B. 400 ml
   C. 600 ml
   D. 1,200 ml
   E. 2,400 ml

33) The average weight of 18 girls in a class is 56 kg and the average weight of 32 boys in the same class is 62 kg. What is the average weight of all the 50 students in that class?
   A. 50
   B. 59.84
   C. 61.68
   D. 61.90
   E. 62.20

34) If the function $g(x)$ has three distinct zeros, which of the following could represent the graph of $g(x)$?

A.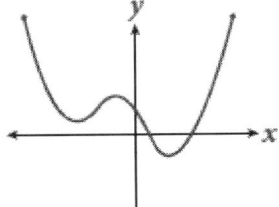

B.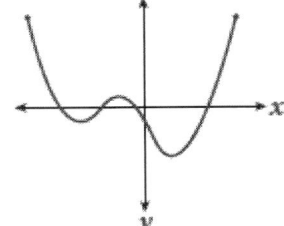

C.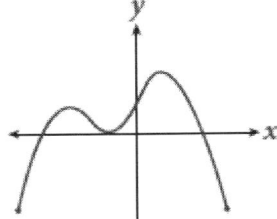

D.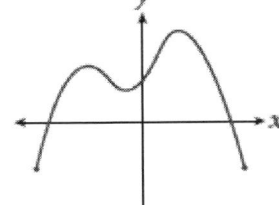

35) If 60% of x equal to 30% of 20, then what is the value of $(x+3)^2$?

   A. 25.25
   B. 26
   C. 26.01
   D. 169
   E. 225

36) Multiply and write the product in scientific notation:
$$(2.9 \times 10^6) \times (2.6 \times 10^{-5})$$
   A. 754×100
   B. 75.4×10^6
   C. 75.4×10^{-5}
   D. 7.54×10^{11}
   E. 7.54×10

37) If the height of a right pyramid is $14\ cm$ and its base is a square with side $6\ cm$. What is its volume?
   A. $432\ cm^3$
   B. $3088\ cm^3$
   C. $236\ cm^3$
   D. $172\ cm^3$
   E. $168\ cm^3$

38) 5 less than twice a positive integer is 73. What is the integer?
   A. 39
   B. 41
   C. 42
   D. 44
   E. 50

39) A shirt costing $300 is discounted 15%. After a month, the shirt is discounted another 15%. Which of the following expressions can be used to find the selling price of the shirt?
   A. $(300)(0.70)$
   B. $(300) - 300(0.30)$
   C. $(300)(0.15) - (300)(0.15)$
   D. $(300)(0.85)(0.85)$
   E. $(300)(0.85)(0.85) - (300)(0.15)$

40) Which of the following points lies on the line $2x + 4y = 8$?
   A. $(2, 1)$
   B. $(-1, 3)$
   C. $(-2, 2)$
   D. $(2, 2)$
   E. $(2, 8)$

41) If $2x + 2y = 2$, $3x - y = 7$, which of the following ordered pairs (x, y) satisfies both equations?
   A. $(1, 3)$
   B. $(2, 4)$
   C. $(2, -1)$
   D. $(4, -6)$
   E. $(1, -6)$

42) If $f(x) = 3x + 4(x + 1) + 2$ then $f(4x) = ?$
   A. $28x + 6$
   B. $16x - 6$
   C. $25x + 4$
   D. $12x + 3$
   E. $12x - 3$

43) A line in the xy-plane passes through origin and has a slope of $\frac{1}{3}$. Which of the following points lies on the line?
   A. $(2, 1)$
   B. $(4, 1)$
   C. $(9, 3)$
   D. $(6, 3)$
   E. $(1, 3)$

44) Which of the following is equivalent to $(3n^2 + 2n + 6) - (2n^2 - 4)$?
   A. $n + 4n^2$
   B. $n^2 - 3$
   C. $n^2 + 2n + 10$
   D. $n + 2$
   E. $n - 2$

45) Solve for x: $4(x + 1) = 6(x - 4) + 20$
   A. 12
   B. 6.5
   C. 4
   D. 2
   E. 0

46) If $x \neq -4$ and $x \neq 5$, which of the following is equivalent to $\dfrac{1}{\frac{1}{x-5}+\frac{1}{x+4}}$?

A. $\dfrac{(x-5)(x+4)}{(x-5)+(x+4)}$

B. $\dfrac{(x+4)+(x-5)}{(x+4)(x-5)}$

C. $\dfrac{(x+4)(x-5)}{(x+4)-(x+5)}$

D. $\dfrac{(x+4)+(x-5)}{(x+4)-(x-5)}$

E. $\dfrac{(x-4)+(x-5)}{(x+4)-(x-5)}$

$$y < c - x, \; y > x + b$$

47) In the xy-plane, if $(0, 0)$ is a solution to the system of inequalities above, which of the following relationships between c and b must be true?

A. $c < b$
B. $c > b$
C. $c = b$
D. $c = b + c$
E. $c = b - x$

48) What is the value of x in the following equation? $3x + 10 = 46$
A. 4
B. 7
C. 10
D. 12
E. 16

49) Calculate $f(5)$ for the following function f.

$$f(x) = x^2 - 3x$$

A. 5

B. 10

C. 15

D. 20

E. 25

50) John buys a pepper plant that is 5 inches tall. With regular watering the plant grows 3 inches a year. Writing John's plant's height as a function of time, what does the y −intercept represent?

   A. The y −intercept represents the rate of grows of the plant which is 5 inches
   B. The y −intercept represents the starting height of 5 inches
   C. The y −intercept represents the rate of growth of plant which is 3 inches per year
   D. The y −intercept is always zero
   E. There is no y −intercept

51) If $\frac{4}{x} = \frac{12}{x-8}$ what is the value of $\frac{x}{2}$?

   A. 1
   B. 3
   C. −2
   D. 2
   E. 0

52) Which of the following is an equation of a circle in the xy-plane with center $(-1, 2)$ and a radius with endpoint $(2, 6)$?

   A. $(x + 1)^2 + (y - 2)^2 = 5$
   B. $2x^2 + (y + 2)^2 = 25$
   C. $(x - 1)^2 + (y - 2)^2 = 5$
   D. $(x + 1)^2 + (y - 2)^2 = 25$
   E. $(x + 1)^2 + (y - 2)^2 = 125$

53) Given a right triangle $\triangle ABC$ whose $\angle B = 90°, \sin C = \frac{8}{17}$, find $\cos A$?

   A. 1
   B. $\frac{8}{15}$
   C. $\frac{8}{17}$
   D. $\frac{15}{17}$
   E. $\frac{1}{8}$

54) The circle graph below shows all Mr. Green's expenses for last month. If he spent $660 on his car, how much did he spend for his rent?

A. $700
B. $740
C. $810
D. $910
E. $960

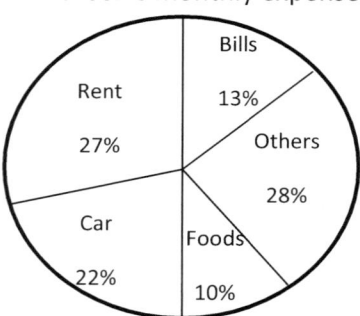
Mr. Green's monthly expenses

55) The Jackson Library is ordering some bookshelves. If x is the number of bookshelves the library wants to order, which each costs $200 and there is a one-time delivery charge of $600, which of the following represents the total cost, in dollar, per bookshelf?

A. $\frac{200x+600}{x}$

B. $\frac{200x+600}{200}$

C. $200 + 600x$

D. $200x + 600$

E. $600x + 600$

56) A function $g(3) = 5$ and $g(5) = 4$. A function $f(5) = 2$ and $f(4) = 6$. What is the value of $f(g(5))$?
A. 5
B. 6
C. 7
D. 8
E. 10

57) What is the area of the following equilateral triangle if the side $AB = 12\ cm$?

A. $36\sqrt{3}\ cm^2$
B. $18\sqrt{3}\ cm^2$
C. $6\sqrt{3}\ cm^2$
D. $8\ cm^2$
E. $6\ cm^2$

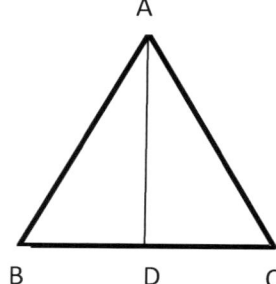

58) If $x \blacksquare y = \sqrt{x^2 + y}$, what is the value of $6 \blacksquare 28$?

   A. $\sqrt{168}$
   B. 10
   C. 8
   D. 6
   E. 4

$$x^2 + y^2 + 8x - 2y = 1$$

59) The equation of a circle in the xy-plane is shown above. What is the radius of the circle?

   A. 24
   B. 18
   C. $\sqrt{18}$
   D. $\sqrt{10}$
   E. $\sqrt{8}$

60) What is the value of y in the following system of equation?

$$3x - 4y = -20$$
$$-x + 2y = 10$$

   A. -1
   B. -2
   C. 1
   D. 4
   E. 5

End of CLEP College Algebra Practice Test

CLEP College Algebra Practice Test

Answers Key

Now, it's time to review your results to see where you went wrong and what areas you need to improve.

| \multicolumn{6}{c}{CLEP College Algebra Practice Test} |

#	Ans	#	Ans	#	Ans
1	B	21	D	41	C
2	D	22	C	42	A
3	D	23	A	43	C
4	E	24	D	44	C
5	E	25	C	45	C
6	E	26	C	46	A
7	E	27	B	47	B
8	D	28	C	48	D
9	B	29	B	49	B
10	C	30	D	50	B
11	B	31	D	51	C
12	D	32	B	52	D
13	E	33	B	53	C
14	B	34	C	54	C
15	C	35	D	55	A
16	C	36	E	56	B
17	A	37	E	57	A
18	E	38	A	58	C
19	D	39	D	59	C
20	A	40	A	60	E

CLEP College Algebra Practice Test

Answers and Explanations

1) Choice B is correct

Plug in each pair of number in the equation:

(2, 1):	2 (2) + 4 (1) = 8	Nope!
(−1, 2):	2 (−1) + 4 (2) = 6	Bingo!
(−2, 2):	2 (−2) + 4 (2) = 4	Nope!
(2, 2):	2 (2) + 4 (2) = 12	Nope!
(2, 8):	2 (2) + 4 (8) = 36	Nope!

2) Choice D is correct

Here we can substitute 8 for x in the equation. Thus, $y - 3 = 2(8 + 5)$, $y - 3 = 26$

Adding 3 to both side f the equation: $y = 26 + 3$, $y = 29$

3) Choice D is correct

Use Pythagorean Theorem: $a^2 + b^2 = c^2 \Rightarrow 5^2 + 12^2 = c^2 \Rightarrow 169 = c^2 \Rightarrow c = 13$

4) Choice E is correct

Th ratio of boy to girls is 2: 3. Therefore, there are 2 boys out of 5 students. To find the answer, first divide the total number of students by 5, then multiply the result by 2.

$500 \div 5 = 100 \Rightarrow 100 \times 2 = 200$

5) Choice E is correct

Use FOIL (First, Out, In, Last). $(7x + 2y)(5x + 2y) = 35x^2 + 14xy + 10xy + 4y^2 =$

$$35x^2 + 24xy + 4y^2$$

6) Choice E is correct

Use distributive property: $5x(4 + 2y) = 20x + 10xy$

7) Choice E is correct

$y = 5ab + 3b^3$. Plug in the values of a and b in the equation: $a = 2$ and $b = 3$.

$y = 5(2)(3) + 3(3)^3 = 30 + 3(27) = 30 + 81 = 111$

8) Choice D is correct

x and z are colinear. y and $5x$ are colinear. Therefore,

$x + z = y + 5x$, subtract x from both sides, then, $z = y + 4x$

9) Choice B is correct

$|x - 10| \leq 3 \rightarrow -3 \leq x - 10 \leq 3 \rightarrow -3 + 10 \leq x - 10 + 10 \leq 3 + 10 \rightarrow 7 \leq x \leq 13$

10) Choice C is correct

Let x be the number. Write the equation and solve for x. $\frac{2}{3} \times 15 = \frac{2}{5} \cdot x \Rightarrow \frac{2 \times 15}{3} = \frac{2x}{5}$, use cross multiplication to solve for x. $5 \times 30 = 2x \times 3 \Rightarrow 150 = 6x \Rightarrow x = 25$

11) Choice B is correct

To find the discount, multiply the number by $(100\% - rate\ of\ discount)$. Therefore, for the first discount we get: $(D)\ (100\% - 25\%) = (D)(0.75) = 0.75$. For increase of 10%: $(0.75\ D)(100\% + 10\%) = (0.75\ D)(1.10) = 0.82\ D = 82\%\ of\ D$ or $0.82\ D$.

12) Choice D is correct

The union of A and B is: $A \cup B = \{1, 2, 3, 4, 5, 6, 11, 15\}$

The intersection of $(A \cup B)$ and C is: $(A \cup B) \cap C = \{5, 11\}$

13) Choice E is correct

$$\text{average} = \frac{\text{sum of terms}}{\text{number of terms}} \Rightarrow 20 = \frac{13 + 15 + 20 + x}{4} \Rightarrow 80 = 48 + x \Rightarrow x = 32$$

14) Choice B is correct

Since $f(x)$ is linear function with a negative slop, then when $x = -2$, $f(x)$ is maximum and when $x = 3$, $f(x)$ is minimum. Then the ratio of the minimum value to the maximum value of the function is: $\frac{f(3)}{f(-2)} = \frac{-3(3)+1}{-3(-2)+1} = \frac{-8}{7} = -\frac{8}{7}$

15) Choice C is correct

There can be 0, 1, or 2 solutions to a quadratic equation. In standard form, a quadratic equation is written as: $ax^2 + bx + c = 0$

For the quadratic equation, the expression $b^2 - 4ac$ is called discriminant. If discriminant is positive, there are 2 distinct solutions for the quadratic equation. If discriminant is 0, there is one solution for the quadratic equation and if it is negative the equation does not have any solutions.

To find number of solutions for $x^2 = 4x - 3$, first, rewrite it as $x^2 - 4x + 3 = 0$.

Find the value of the discriminant. $b^2 - 4ac = (-4)^2 - 4(1)(3) = 16 - 12 = 4$

Since the discriminant is positive, the quadratic equation has two distinct solutions.

16) Choice C is correct

If the value of $|x - 3| + 3$ is equal to 0, then $|x - 3| + 3 = 0$. Subtracting 3 from both sides of this equation gives $|x - 3| = -3$. The expression $|x - 3|$ on the left side of the equation is the absolute value of $x - 3$, and the absolute value can never be a negative number.

Thus $|x - 3| = -3$ has no solution. Therefore, there are no values for x for which the value of $|x - 3| + 3$ is equal to 0.

17) Choice A is correct

Let x be the number of years. Therefore, $2,000 per year equals $2000x$. starting from $26,000 annual salary means you should add that amount to $2000x$. Income more than that is:

$I > 2000 x + 26000$

18) Choice E is correct

Use the information provided in the question to draw the shape.

Use Pythagorean Theorem: $a^2 + b^2 = c^2$

$60^2 + 80^2 = c^2 \Rightarrow 3600 + 6400 = c^2 \Rightarrow 10000 = c^2 \Rightarrow c = 100$

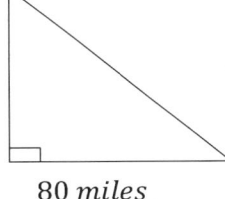

60 miles

80 miles

19) Choice D is correct

In the figure angle A is labeled $(3x - 2)$ and it measures 37. Thus, $3x - 2 = 37$ and $3x = 39$ or $x = 13$. That means that angle B, which is labeled $(5x)$, must measure $5 \times 13 = 65$.

Since the three angles of a triangle must add up to 180, $37 + 65 + y - 8 = 180$, then:

$$y + 94 = 108 \rightarrow y = 180 - 94 = 86$$

20) Choice A is correct

If the score of Mia was 40, therefore the score of Ava is 20. Since, the score of Emma was half as that of Ava, therefore, the score of Emma is 10.

21) Choice D is correct

The union of A and B is: $A \cup B = \{1, 2, 4, 8, 12, 16, 24, 32, 48\}$. There are 9 elements in $A \cup B$.

22) Choice C is correct

Let x be the smallest number. Then, these are the numbers: $x, x + 1, x + 2, x + 3, x + 4$

average $= \frac{\text{sum of terms}}{\text{number of terms}} \Rightarrow 36 = \frac{x+(x+1)+(x+2)+(x+3)+(x+4)}{5} \Rightarrow 36 = \frac{5x+10}{5} \Rightarrow$

$$180 = 5x + 10 \Rightarrow 170 = 5x \Rightarrow x = 34$$

23) Choice A is correct

Subtracting $2x$ and adding 5 to both sides of $2x - 5 \geq 3x - 1$ gives $-4 \geq x$. Therefore, x is a solution to $2x - 5 \geq 3x - 1$ if and only if x is less than or equal to -4 and x is NOT a solution to $2x - 5 \geq 3x - 1$ if and only if x is greater than -4. Of the choices given, only -2 is greater than -4 and, therefore, cannot be a value of x.

24) Choice D is correct

Given the two equations, substitute the numerical value of a into the second equation to solve for x. $a = \sqrt{3}$, $4a = \sqrt{4x}$

Substituting the numerical value for a into the equation with x is as follows.

$4(\sqrt{3}) = \sqrt{4x}$, From here, distribute the 4. $4\sqrt{3} = \sqrt{4x}$

Now square both side of the equation. $(4\sqrt{3})^2 = (\sqrt{4x})^2$

Remember to square both terms within the parentheses. Also, recall that squaring a square root sign cancels them out. $4^2\sqrt{3}^2 = 4x$, $16(3) = 4x$, $48 = 4x$, $x = 12$

25) Choice C is correct

First square both sides of the equation to get $4m - 3 = m^2$

Subtracting both sides by $4m - 3$ gives us the equation $m^2 - 4m + 3 = 0$

Here you can solve the quadratic equation by factoring to get $(m - 1)(m - 3) = 0$

For the expression $(m - 1)(m - 3)$ to equal zero, $m = 1$ or $m = 3$

26) Choice C is correct

Let x be the number. Write the equation and solve for x. $(28 - x) \div x = 3$

Multiply both sides by x. $(28 - x) = 3x$, then add x both sides. $28 = 4x$, now divide both sides by 4. $x = 7$

27) Choice B is correct

The sum of supplement angles is 180. Let x be that angle. Therefore, $x + 9x = 180$

$10x = 180$, divide both sides by 10: $x = 18$

28) Choice C is correct

First square both sides of the equation to get $4m - 3 = m^2$

Subtracting both sides by $4m - 3$ gives us the equation $m^2 - 4m + 3 = 0$

Here you can solve the quadratic equation by factoring to get $(m - 1)(m - 3) = 0$

For the expression $(m - 1)(m - 3)$ to equal zero, $m = 1$ or $m = 3$

29) Choice B is correct

$$tan\theta = \frac{opposite}{adjacent}$$

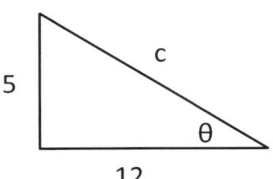

$tan\theta = \frac{5}{12} \Rightarrow$ we have the following right triangle. Then

$c = \sqrt{5^2 + 12^2} = \sqrt{25 + 144} = \sqrt{169} = 13$

$cos\theta = \frac{adjacent}{hypotenuse} = \frac{12}{13}$

30) Choice D is correct

The amplitude in the graph of the equation $y = a cos bx$ is a. (a and b are constant)

In the equation $y = cos x$, the amplitude is 2 and the period of the graph is 2π.

The only choice that has two times the amplitude of graph $y = cos\ x$ is $y = 2 + 2\ cos\ x$

They both have the amplitude of 2 and period of 2π.

31) Choice D is correct

Substituting 6 for x and 14 for y in $y = nx + 2$ gives $14 = (n)(6) + 2$,

which gives $n = 2$. Hence, $y = 2x + 2$. Therefore, when $x = 10$, the value of y is

$$y = (2)(10) + 2 = 22.$$

32) Choice B is correct

6% of the volume of the solution is alcohol. Let x be the volume of the solution.

Then: $6\%\ of\ x = 24\ ml \Rightarrow 0.06\ x = 24 \Rightarrow x = 24 \div 0.06 = 400$

33) Choice B is correct

average $= \frac{sum\ of\ terms}{number\ of\ terms}$. The sum of the weight of all girls is: $18 \times 56 = 1,008\ kg$

The sum of the weight of all boys is: $32 \times 62 = 1,984\ kg$. The sum of the weight of all students is: $1,008 + 1,984 = 2,992\ kg$. average $= \frac{2992}{50} = 59.84$

34) Choice C is correct

A zero of a function corresponds to an x-intercept of the graph of the function in the xy-plane. Therefore, the graph of the function $g(x)$, which has three distinct zeros, must have three x-intercepts. Only the graph in choice C has three x-intercepts.

35) Choice D is correct

$0.6x = (0.3) \times 20 \rightarrow x = 10 \rightarrow (x+3)^2 = (13)^2 = 169$

36) Choice E is correct

$(2.9 \times 10^6) \times (2.6 \times 10^{-5}) = (2.9 \times 2.6) \times (10^6 \times 10^{-5}) = 7.54 \times (10^{6+(-5)})$
$= 7.54 \times 10^1$

37) Choice E is correct

The formula of the volume of pyramid is: $V = \frac{l \times w \times h}{3}$

The length and width of the pyramid is 6 cm and its height is 14 cm. Therefore:

$$V = \frac{6 \times 6 \times 14}{3} = 168 \ cm^3$$

38) Choice A is correct

Let x be the integer. Then: $2x - 5 = 73$, Add 5 both sides: $2x = 78$, Divide both sides by 2:

$$x = 39$$

39) Choice D is correct

To find the discount, multiply the number by $(100\% - ate\ of\ discount)$. Therefore, for the first discount we get: $(300)(100\% - 15\%) = (300)(0.85)$. For the next 15% discount: $(300)(0.85)(0.85)$.

40) Choice A is correct

Plug in each pair of number in the equation: $2x + 4y = 8$

A. $(2, 1)$: $2(2) + 4(1) = 8$
B. $(-1, 3)$: $2(-1) + 4(3) = 10$
C. $(-2, 2)$: $2(-2) + 4(2) = 4$
D. $(2, 2)$: $2(2) + 4(2) = 12$
E. $(2, 8)$: $2(2) + 4(8) = 36$

Only choice A is correct.

41) Choice C is correct

Plugin the values of x and y provided in the choices into both equations. Let's start with $2x + 2y = 2$:

A. (1, 3) $2x + 2y = 2 \to 2 + 6 \neq 2$
B. (2, 4) $2x + y = 2 \to 4 + 8 \neq 2$
C. (2, −1) $2x + 2y = 2 \to 4 + (−2) = 2$
D. (4, −6) $2x + 2y = 2 \to 12 + (−12) \neq 2$
E. (1, −6) $2x + 2y = 2 \to 2 + (−12) \neq 2$

Only choice C is correct.

42) Choice A is correct

If $f(x) = 3x + 4(x + 1) + 2$, then find $f(4x)$ by substituting $4x$ for every x in the function. This gives: $f(4x) = 3(4x) + 4(4x + 1) + 2$

It simplifies to: $f(4x) = 3(4x) + 4(4x + 1) + 2 = 12x + 16x + 4 + 2 = 28x + 6$

43) Choice C is correct

First, find the equation of the line. All lines through the origin are of the form $y = mx$, so the equation is $y = \frac{1}{3}x$. Of the given choices, only choice C (9,3), satisfies this equation:
$y = \frac{1}{3}x \to 3 = \frac{1}{3}(9) = 3$

44) Choice C is correct

$(3n^2 + 2n + 6) − (2n^2 − 4)$. Add like terms together: $3n^2 − 2n^2 = n^2$, $2n$ doesn't have like terms. $6 − (−4) = 10$, Combine these terms into one expression to find the answer: $n^2 + 2n + 10$

45) Choice C is correct

Simplify and solve for x in the equation. $4(x + 1) = 6(x − 4) + 20$, $4x + 4 = 6x − 24 + 20$, $4x + 4 = 6x − 4$. Subtract $4x$ from both sides: $4 = 2x − 4$, Add 4 to both sides: $8 = 2x$, $4 = x$

46) Choice A is correct

To rewrite $\frac{1}{\frac{1}{x-5}+\frac{1}{x+4}}$, first simplify $\frac{1}{x-5} + \frac{1}{x+4}$.

$\frac{1}{x-5} + \frac{1}{x+4} = \frac{1(x+4)}{(x-5)(x+4)} + \frac{1(x-5)}{(x+4)(x-5)} = \frac{(x+4)+(x-5)}{(x+4)(x-5)}$

Then: $\frac{1}{\frac{1}{x-5}+\frac{1}{x+4}} = \frac{1}{\frac{(x+4)+(x-5)}{(x+4)(x-5)}} = \frac{(x-5)(x+4)}{(x-5)+(x+4)}$. (Remember, $\frac{1}{\frac{1}{x}} = x$)

This result is equivalent to the expression in choice A.

47) Choice B is correct

Since $(0, 0)$ is a solution to the system of inequalities, substituting 0 for x and 0 for y in the given system must result in two true inequalities. After this substitution, $y < c − x$ becomes $0 < a$, and $y > x + b$ becomes $0 > b$. Hence, a is positive and b is negative.
Therefore, $c > b$.

48) Choice D is correct

$3x + 10 = 46 \rightarrow 3x = 46 - 10 = 36 \rightarrow x = \frac{36}{3} = 12$

49) Choice B is correct

The input value is 5. Then: $x = 5$. $f(x) = x^2 - 3x \rightarrow f(5) = 5^2 - 3(5) = 25 - 15 = 10$

50) Choice B is correct

To solve this problem, first recall the equation of a line: $y = mx + b$

Where $m = slope$. $y = y - intercept$

Remember that slope is the rate of change that occurs in a function and that the y-intercept is the y value corresponding to $x = 0$.

Since the height of John's plant is 5 inches tall when he gets it. Time (or x) is zero. The plant grows 3 inches per year. Therefore, the rate of change of the plant's height is 3. The y-intercept represents the starting height of the plant which is 5 inches.

51) Choice C is correct

Multiplying each side of $\frac{4}{x} = \frac{12}{x-8}$ by $x(x - 8)$ gives $4(x - 8) = 12(x)$, distributing the 4 over the values within the parentheses yields $x - 8 = 3x$ or $x = -4$.

Therefore, the value of $\frac{x}{2} = \frac{-4}{2} = -2$.

52) Choice D is correct

The equation of a circle can be written as $(x - h)^2 + (y - k)^2 = r^2$
where (h, k) are the coordinates of the center of the circle and r is the radius of the circle. Since the coordinates of the center of the circle are $(-1, 2)$, the equation is
$(x + 1)^2 + (y - 2)^2 = r^2$, where r is the radius. The radius of the circle is the distance from the center $(-1, 2)$, to the given endpoint of a radius, $(2, 6)$. By the distance formula,
$$r^2 = (2 - (-1))^2 + (6 - 2)^2 = (3)^2 + (4)^2 = 9 + 16 = 25$$
Therefore, an equation of the given circle is $(x + 1)^2 + (y - 2)^2 = 25$

53) Choice C is correct

To solve for $\cos A$ first identify what is known. The question states that $\triangle ABC$ is a right triangle whose $\angle B = 90°$ and $\sin C = \frac{8}{17}$.

It is important to recall that any triangle has a sum of interior angles that equals 180 degrees. Therefore, to calculate $\cos A$ use the complimentary angles identify of trigonometric function. $\cos A = \cos(90 - C)$,   Then: $\cos A = \sin C$

For complementary angles, sin of one angle is equal to cos of the other angle. $\cos A = \frac{2}{3}$

54) Choice C is correct

Let x be all expenses, then $\frac{22}{100}x = \$660 \rightarrow x = \frac{100 \times \$660}{22} = \$3,000$

Mr. Jones spent for his rent: $\frac{27}{100} \times \$3{,}000 = \$810$

55) Choice A is correct

The amount of money for x bookshelf is: $200x$, Then, the total cost of all bookshelves is equal to: $200x + 600$, The total cost, in dollar, per bookshelf is: $\frac{Total\ cost}{number\ of\ items} = \frac{200x+600}{x}$

56) Choice B is correct

It is given that $g(5) = 4$. Therefore, to find the value of $f(g(5))$, then $f(g(5)) = f(4) = 6$

57) Choice A is correct

Area of the triangle is: $\frac{1}{2} AD \times BC$ and AD is perpendicular to BC. Triangle ADC is a $30° - 60° - 90°$ right triangle. The relationship among all sides of right triangle $30° - 60° - 90°$ is provided in the following triangle: In this triangle, the opposite side of 30° angle is half of the hypotenuse. And the opposite side of 60° is opposite of 30° × $\sqrt{3}$

$CD = 6$, then $AD = 6 \times \sqrt{3}$

Area of the triangle ABC is: $\frac{1}{2} AD \times BC = \frac{1}{2} 6\sqrt{3} \times 12 = 36\sqrt{3}$

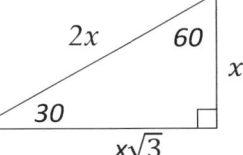

58) Choice C is correct

$6 \blacksquare 28 = \sqrt{6^2 + 28} = \sqrt{36 + 28} = \sqrt{64} = 8$

59) Choice C is correct

The equation of a circle with center (h, k) and radius r is $(x - h)^2 + (y - k)^2 = r^2$. To put the equation $x^2 + y^2 + 8x - 2y = 1$ in this form, complete the square as follows:

$x^2 + y^2 + 8x - 2y = 1$, $(x^2 + 8x) + (y^2 - 2y) = 1$

$(x^2 + 8x + 16) - 16 + (y^2 - 2y + 1) - 1 = 1$, $(x + 4)^2 + (y - 1)^2 = 18$

$(x + 4)^2 + (y - 1)^2 = (\sqrt{18})^2$

Therefore, the radius of the circle is $\sqrt{18}$.

60) Choice E is correct

Solve the system of equations by elimination method.

$3x - 4y = -20$
$-x + 2y = 10$ Multiply the second equation by 3, then add it to the first equation.

$\begin{matrix} 3x - 4y = -20 \\ 3(-x + 2y = 10) \end{matrix} \Rightarrow \begin{matrix} 3x - 4y = -20 \\ -3x + 6y = 30 \end{matrix} \Rightarrow$ add the equations $2y = 10 \Rightarrow y = 5$

"Effortless Math" Publications

Effortless Math authors' team strives to prepare and publish the best quality CLEP College Algebra learning resources to make learning Math easier for all. We hope that our publications help you learn Math in an effective way and prepare for the CLEP College Algebra test.

We all in Effortless Math wish you good luck and successful studies!

Effortless Math Authors

www.EffortlessMath.com

... So Much More Online!

✓ FREE Math lessons

✓ More Math learning books!

✓ Mathematics Worksheets

✓ Online Math Tutors

Need a PDF version of this book?

Please visit www.EffortlessMath.com

Made in the USA
Columbia, SC
20 February 2021